Corporate Codes of Conduct

An Examination and Implementation Guide

by

Stephen Landekich

Report on a research project commissioned by
National Association of Accountants
Montvale, New Jersey

Published by

National Association of Accountants
10 Paragon Drive
Montvale, NJ 07645-1760
Claire Barth, Editor

NAA Publication Number 89237
ISBN 0-86641-175-5

Foreword

In December 1985 Jack Krogstad, director of research of the National Commission on Fraudulent Financial Reporting (NCFFR), and Dewey Arnold, executive director of the Commission, presented the Commission's research needs to staff of the National Association of Accountants (NAA), among them Steve Landekich, director of management accounting practices. After discussion as to the topic, the staff proposed to sponsor research about codes of conduct applied by professional groups and corporations. Mr. Landekich was asked to conduct the study.

In July 1986, the NCFFR discussed the results of his report, titled "Impact of Professionalism and Codes of Corporate Conduct on Financial Reporting." As stated on page 10[1] of the October 1987 report of the Commission, "this study describes and analyzes two predominant ethical forces that come to bear on the financial reporting process — the corporate ethical climate and professional codes of ethics." Examining both of the forces, "the study also cautions that while improved accounting and auditing standards may help independent public accountants prevent and detect fraudulent financial reporting, these are not substitutes for a willingness to place professional ethics above the pressures of the accounting marketplace."

Because this study was aimed specifically at the needs of the NCFFR and not written in the style normally publishable by NAA, NAA then requested the same researcher, Steve Landekich, to prepare a proposal for a follow-up study that would:

1. Extend the research,
2. Draft a model ethical code of conduct for corporations, and
3. Develop the manuscript in a format suitable for publication by NAA.

The Committee on Research subsequently approved this proposal at its January 8, 1987, meeting.

While this "report centers on the ethics-oriented efforts that should be on the agenda of every company," it offers practical guidance for the implementation of a code of ethics in the corporate environment.

Small and medium-sized corporations should find the final chapter on recommendations for preparing a corporate code of ethics very helpful. This study contributes to the body of knowledge and practices of management accounting.

Guidance in the preparation of the research was kindly provided by the Project Committee:

Thomas H. Williams, *Chairman*
University of Wisconsin
Madison, Wisconsin

Neil Holmes   Mark E. Rennhack
The Marley Company   Glaxo, Inc.
Mission Woods, Kansas   Research Triangle Park, North Carolina

The report reflects the views of the researcher and not necessarily those of the Association, the Committee on Research, or the Project Committee.

Patrick L. Romano
Director of Research
National Association of Accountants

Acknowledgments

I appreciate the support of the NAA Committee on Research. Valuable advice was received from the Project Committee chaired by Dr. Thomas H. Williams (University of Wisconsin), whose guidance was extremely helpful.

The Treadway Commission's treatment of my work was highly encouraging. Among others whose favorable opinions meant very much to me were Donald W. Baker (Southwire Company), then chairman of the NAA Committee on Research, and Howard L. Siers (DuPont de Nemours), chairman of the NAA Ad Hoc Committee on Ethics. Mr. Siers also contributed suggestions later in the project.

The strong supportive response from a substantial proportion of the corporate executives contacted in the course of the project was especially meaningful and gratifying. They shared with me their in-house company materials, providing the documentation essential to the research quality of the project design. They described and assessed their ethics-related experience, explained company policies, and articulated their personal views. Many also offered further participation in the research. I am particularly appreciative of the support given me by Chairman Edmund T. Pratt, Jr. (Pfizer Inc.) and Fred S. Schulte (Tracor, Inc.).

A debt of gratitude is owed to the many, known and unknown, whose efforts are reflected in codes of ethics or similar corporate policies, to the authors and publishers of works on ethics, and to all the ethics activists whose thoughts enabled me to reach the degree of insight needed for this project. I am indebted to Dana Corporation, Johnson & Johnson, and to other grantors of reprint permissions. Much of the discussion presented in this report relies on responses from various anonymous companies, included in the initial sample or contacted subsequently. Some of the replies were used in preparing samples or exhibits.

I would like to express my appreciation to the staff of the NAA, especially to Alfred M. King, managing director of professional services, for his firm confidence and active support throughout the project; to Patrick L. Romano, director of research, for his guidance in preparing the final draft; to Kim Barbagallo for her able assistance at the beginning of the project; and to Claire Barth, associate editor, for taking care of editorial and publication matters with knowledgeable effectiveness.

About the Author

Stephen Landekich is now self-employed. He worked for 27 years with the National Association of Accountants, first as editor of MANAGEMENT ACCOUNTING and then as director of research and director of the Management Accounting Practices Committee. His books and articles on economics, accounting, organization and control, and commercial operations have been published in both his native Yugoslavia and the United States.

Mr. Landekich holds a diploma in economics from Zagreb University (Yugoslavia) and an MBA degree in economic theory.

Table of Contents

Figures

Executive Summary

This report contains no spectacular revelations nor impressive findings that offer a new, painless cure to company ethical problems. The report does show both the need for and benefits of company attempts to operate at a high level of ethics, at a level where a company's reputation and the related competitive edge are less vulnerable, less exposed to sudden shocks and setbacks of an ethical nature.

In general, the report centers on the ethics-oriented efforts that should be on the agenda of every company. The report is organized to present ethics as a resource no company can afford to neglect, a resource that is especially valuable to a company whose management would like to rise above mediocrity.

Introduction

The themes of this chapter broaden gradually as the discussion progresses — from ethics as a source of personal strength in the first section to corporate ethical climate in the second section and ethical climate in general in the third section.

The center section on corporate ethical climate outlines the roles of corporate management, professional employees, and the internal auditing function.

The concluding section deals with corporate ethics problems in the context of overall societal conditions and trends. It gives illustrations of fraudulent practices and corresponding concerns. One of the immediate effects of these widespread practices and concerns is heightened ethical sensitivity in our society. The other is the increasing recognition by corporate managements that no company can afford to remain complacent as to the ethical side of its activities.

Research Purposes and Methods

Three of the four sections in this chapter describe the project, research design, and research sample. The last section covers research methods other than those used in this project.

The description of the work on the project includes references to the earlier report prepared for the Treadway Commission and also a condensed set of recommendations presented to the Commission in that report.

Concepts and Perceptions of Business Ethics

The central theme is the role of business in our society. Business ethics is often conceived and assessed principally in terms of its responsibilities to meet certain expectations regarding business support for numerous worthy causes. The proponents of such a view at the same time are opposed to all manifestations of business power when it is not used for their favorite purposes.

One section, on social impact, deals with the NAA taxonomy developed by a committee in 1973. The committee identified four principal areas of corporate performance and provided a comprehensive list of "typical examples," which is shown in its entirety.

Business Ethics as Seen by Corporations

While the preceding chapter discussed the role of business as seen by various parties, this chapter analyzes business ethics in corporate practice. It also presents differing company positions toward codes of ethics.

The chapter begins with symbolism and loyalty as a means of achieving ethics in corporate cultures and ends with views expressed by corporate managements.

Main Types of Ethics Policy Statements

Diverse practices are evident in corporate statements. The author has classified them into three main types, according to the extent and way they deal with the subject of corporate ethics.

Each of the types is presented in a separate section. The full text of a corporate statement illustrates the general policy statement approach. The responsibility/commitment approach is treated similarly but more extensively. The concluding section gives a brief exposition of the standards-of-ethics approach.

Corporate Codes of Ethics

The author describes codes of ethics received from research sample companies and identifies and discusses their main characteristics. Sections on ethics programs and implementation/compliance subject areas follow.

Policies on conflicts of interest take a prominent place in many of the codes of ethics, which is one reason they are given in a separate section with several illustrations. Another reason for treating them separately is the author's view that those policies should be issued separately rather than within codes of ethics.

Corporate Records and Reports

The input into a corporate database can be the original source of many errors and improprieties. In general, the description of the process of preparing corporate financial statements mainly covers integrity of financial reporting.

A section deals with fraudulent reporting, followed by an analysis of "earnings-management" practices.

Corporate Disclosure System

The corporate disclosure system is treated here in the context of corporate governance issues. Some questionable voting/decision structures and management practices that may not be consistent with fiduciary duties may cause ethical concern. The next two sections cover various forms of communications used in the disclosure system and the role of principal participants in this segment of corporate activity.

In the concluding section, we review the current status of efforts to remove unwarranted differences in financial reporting among countries. The ethics implications also are explored.

Recommendations

This final chapter is intended to provide direct practical guidance and assistance. It shows how to prepare and implement codes of ethics, how to take care of compliance monitoring, why some actions should or should not be taken, which preliminary considerations should govern the effort, and what should be included in codes of ethics. The recommendations cover all matters of relevance in company decisions and actions regarding their current or future codes of ethics. The centerpiece is a complete code of ethics. It contains "core" standards applicable to codes of ethics of many companies. Possible modifications also are presented and explained.

Chapter 1

Introduction

Ethics Makes Us Stronger

Ethics, first of all, gives the ability to recognize ethical conflicts and dilemmas — situations involving a right-wrong or a proper-improper distinction. This is the cornerstone of an ethical approach whenever we have to choose among two or more conflicting courses of action.

Our sense of ethics provides basic guidance as to the ethically acceptable alternatives. It also points us toward the best solution and may give us the strength to make a proper choice even under adverse circumstances. Of course, ethics does not operate in a vacuum, if a person lacks adequate knowledge, objectivity, and independent judgment.

A person's competence and objectivity are the roots of ethical performance. As to independence, it is not necessary to have the status of an external auditor to make independent ethical judgments. After all, our company management may be urging us, to borrow a phrase, "to take the high road." This should be sufficient, as long as the announced principle remains a regular standard of conduct observed in the company's practice.

Under adverse circumstances, our choice may reflect the influence of corporate ethics on our behavior or, in other words, on our level of ethics. We may find it sensible or prudent to accept a compromise that does not meet our own standards but is still within a satisfactory range, that is, it is not unethical. In repeated situations of this type, employees often have to adjust their personal ethics accordingly. When the employees simultaneously are urged to follow the "highest" ethical standards, the adjustment process becomes more difficult because they perceive the high-ethics pronouncements or policies as a contradiction or hypocrisy.

1

As a rule, an employee (other than a CEO) cannot refuse to go along with the prevailing standards of conduct unless he or she is able and willing to take the negative consequences. An employee does not have to become a "whistle blower" to experience them sooner or later—if he or she is still there.

Corporate Resource

Ethics is a corporate resource. It could be considered plain common sense and could be included among any of the work-performance characteristics that a company requires of its "human resources."

One may assume, therefore, that ethics does not have to be considered separately, as a human characteristic or as an organizational and managerial issue. Proper hiring practices, competitive levels of compensation, performance incentives, company tradition and reputation, control mechanisms, and other similar attributes of the corporate structure and pattern of activities would seem sufficient to assure a standard level of conduct by the employees, managers included.

Ethics does not lend itself to the accounting process of measurement as an item separate from other resources. Anything measurable is, rather, an expense—the effort spent on an active ethics program. But ethics, or the lack of it, does make costs higher or lower, the quality of products higher or lower, both the production volume and the resulting revenues higher or lower. In a service business, the underlying ethics can be even more critical.

The state of ethics affects a company's capacity to conduct its affairs in a lawful manner and to meet the expectations of its shareholders and other constituencies. In other words, ethics is a quality ingredient in the fabric of business.

Our approach here is to treat ethics as a means of achieving better performance and, ultimately, a means of attaining a higher quality of life.

Corporate Ethical Climate

Ethics at Work

We use the term "corporate ethical climate" to denote the totality of business ethics at work in a company. It is an aggregate indicator of the prevailing ethics-related factors within a company. The ethical climate, whatever its strength or level, affects our personal sense of ethics, though we may not always recognize the ethical dilemmas or be able to evaluate all of their ramifications so as to maintain a consistent standard of ethical conduct.

A business enterprise functions through purposeful and continuing activities that involve a number of individuals. The level of ethics prevailing at an employee's work place is an important determinant of the company's strength.

An employee's work place may be thousands of miles away from the corporate office, but the respective behavioral patterns, in terms of ethics, may be very similar. This phenomenon has been used constructively and effectively by many companies that nourish the notions of corporate culture and employee loyalty.

Corporate ethical climate sometimes is interpreted in terms of regimentation rather than ethics. A "top-down" approach of this type often increases work pressures and creates new ethical dilemmas. It expands company demands instead of strengthening ethical leadership by its management.

As an illustration, let us quote a few passages from Peter F. Drucker's "New Age Sessions Are Same Old Brainwashing" (*The Wall Street Journal*, February 9, 1989, p. A20):

> Another wave of pop-psychology is hitting American management. Business after business is putting its managers into 'New Age' seminars...All promise 'consciousness-raising' and non-religious conversion resulting in a 'changed person.'
> ...In the late '20s and early '30s, managements became infatuated with auto-hypnosis...In the late '50s and early '60s, we had the 'sensitivity training' of 'T-groups.' Now we have 'consciousness-raising.'
> ...All these methods use pretty much the same technique.
> ...The crucial issue when employees are ordered into such sessions is, however, neither efficacy nor the potential to do damage. It is the morality and, indeed, even the legality of the practice... 'consciousness-raising' is abuse of power. However well meant, it is brainwashing.

The Role of Corporate Management

It is the responsibility of a company management, in its leadership function, to behave in a manner above reproach in all business affairs, personal and corporate. Executives are entitled to certain benefits and privileges as well as considerable powers commensurate with their positions and not shared equally by other employees. Their ethical behavior is a prime corresponding responsibility. They should be expected not only to act at the highest level of ethics but also to be aware particularly of the appearance and perceptions that their actions create. No one, especially a member of the top management team, should ever be exempt from any rule of ethics that is applicable, explicitly or implicitly, to the others in the company.

A company's managers should consider the organizational structure, as well as their own managerial style, from an ethical point of view — along with other relevant factors, of course. For example, no employees should be exposed unduly to excessive ethical risks, by being assigned responsibilities or otherwise being placed in positions involving ethical dilemmas beyond their capacity to resolve at the expected level of ethical conduct.

The vital role of ethics becomes dramatically evident in cases of fraudulent and unethical behavior that cause damage to the company's property, reputation, and performance, as well as to the ethical climate. It is likely that the company management's watchful awareness of the overall ethical status will enable it to take corrective actions in time and thus reduce the frequency and/or magnitude of any destructive activities. Such responsibilities remain a part of each manager's job regardless of the mechanisms designated specifically for control purposes.

A desirable level of the corporate ethical climate depends on the stability and continuity of favorable conditions. Drastic remedies, such as disciplinary actions for violations of the standards or sudden ethical edicts and announcements, take time to be perceived and accepted as lasting changes in the ethical climate.

Ethics is a resource that cannot be depleted. It invigorates a business enterprise and yet costs so little, except possibly in terms of the management's own behavior. Ethics is not a resource to be used; it has to be lived.

The Role of Professional Employees

Professionalism generally means that a person acts and is expected to act as an expert at a reliable level of conduct. In other words, both competence and integrity are essential.

A professional not only acts in a manner beyond reproach but also is careful about any related conditions and circumstances that possibly might appear improper or be so perceived by others. Consequently, a code of ethics is a distinct mark of an established profession.

Professional codes of ethics also apply, as appropriate, to those professionals who work as company employees. Some ethical responsibilities apply only to the professionals in independent public practice, such as CPAs performing independent audits, and are not entirely applicable to CPAs who are company employees. In all other respects, companies are entitled to expect that professional employees will perform their company functions in conformance with the codes of ethics of their professions.

Companies normally expect professional persons not only to sustain the established corporate ethical climate but also to assume leadership roles through their exemplary behavior. Some professional employees, such as those holding managerial or supervisory positions or those providing legal, accounting, and auditing services, have additional ethics-related responsibilities.

Internal Auditing

In the context of this study, activities of internal auditors are of crucial importance. As a rule, an internal audit unit functions as an independent control arm of top management. With respect to questions related to audit matters, internal auditing also reports directly to the audit committee of the board of directors.

To preserve independence, objectivity, and impartiality of the internal audit unit, internal auditors have no responsibility for any operations of the company. They occasionally, however, do get work assignments to prepare various analyses or proposals, especially in smaller companies. In general, it does not seem advisable to burden internal auditors with any nonaudit work. The control function usually is interpreted to include recommendations based on audit findings.

Internal auditors have complete access to all records, property, and personnel relevant to the performance of their duties and responsibilities. Internal auditors also have full and independent access to all levels of management and the audit committee. All employees are required to provide full support to internal auditors and do whatever is necessary to facilitate their work. A major role of internal auditors is to cooperate with independent public auditors at all times.

Effectiveness of company internal auditing is the mainstay of a favorable corporate ethical climate. Internal auditors also have a major role in the monitoring and enforcement of company codes of ethics.

Almost all companies participating in our survey have one or more policies on internal auditing, usually set forth in considerable detail. Many companies also state auditing standards and interpret them.

The code adopted by the Institute of Internal Auditors outlines the standards of the profession for the guidance of the Institute's members who "represent the profession of internal auditing." The code is composed of: Introduction, Interpretation of Principles, and eight Articles. Article VI deals with a matter of vital concern — audit reports:

> VI. Members, in expressing an opinion, shall use all reasonable care to obtain sufficient factual evidence to warrant such expression. In their reporting, members shall reveal such material facts known to them, which, if not revealed, could distort the report of the results of operations under review or conceal unlawful practice.

Ethical Climate in General

Work-Related Ethical Dilemmas

In our complex society, a rather intricate web of work relationships has become a regular feature in many a field of activity, especially at the upper levels. It is not unusual for an individual to experience conflict-of-interest situations.

All too familiar is the "revolving door" practice involving former government officials working later for defense contractors. On numerous occasions in the recent past, most of us also learned of peculiar circumstantial evidence concerning the objectivity of various "independent" experts.

Some types of professional activities provide opportunities for ethical conflicts with far-reaching consequences. The ethical exposure present in the company-researcher relationships has been recognized widely in medical research. As disclosed in "Bad Chemistry" by Marilyn Chase (*The Wall Street Journal*, January 26, 1989, pp. A1 and A6), "the perfectly legal practice of researchers acquiring stock in drug companies has become so widespread, critics say, that it threatens the atmosphere of scientific inquiry." Her concluding paragraph seems to be of particular relevance:

> Pioneering TPA researcher Eric Topol of the University of Michigan at Ann Arbor also wrestled with temptation, but remains stock-free. About a year ago, Genentech sent him options to buy 1,000 shares. He weighed the offer for a while, but growing increasingly uncomfortable, shipped the unused options back to the company. His one regret: 'I should have sent them back the day they arrived.'

Among the conspicuous factors incompatible with a high level of ethical climate in general is the frequency of fraud. As an illustration, we present statistics in Figure 1 on arrests in 1976-1986 for "white-collar" embezzlement and fraud.

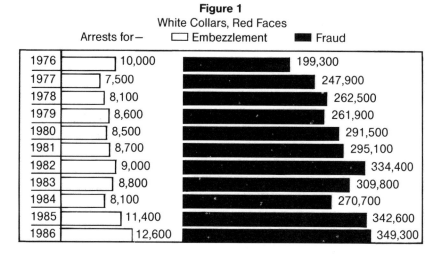

Figure 1
White Collars, Red Faces
Arrests for— ☐ Embezzlement ▉ Fraud

Year	Embezzlement	Fraud
1976	10,000	199,300
1977	7,500	247,900
1978	8,100	262,500
1979	8,600	261,900
1980	8,500	291,500
1981	8,700	295,100
1982	9,000	334,400
1983	8,800	309,800
1984	8,100	270,700
1985	11,400	342,600
1986	12,600	349,300

Ethics 101

How do you figure it? Arrests in the U.S. for two categories of white-collar crimes have climbed: Fraud jumped 75 percent between 1976 and 1986, and embezzlement rose 26 percent. Yet business experts and members of Congress ranked U.S. professional ethics first in the world. Countries like Germany and Japan placed much lower. Could artistic impression be triumphing over technical merit?

Note: Fraud—obtaining money or property under false pretenses—includes shoplifting, bad checks, leaving without paying, confidence games, unauthorized withdrawals from ATM machines and computer crimes. Embezzlement is defined as the misappropriation of money or property entrusted to you, or an attempt at misappropriation.

USN&WR—Basic data: Federal Bureau of Investigation.

Compiled by Michael H. Gallagher, Jo Ann Tooley, Marianna I. Knight, Andrew Turner and Edwina Anderson

Adapted from *U.S. News & World Report,* March 14, 1988, p. 76. Copyright, 1988, *U.S. News & World Report.* Used by permission.

Company-wide Ethical Exposure

Consider, for example, one of the three "scandal" cases described in "Businesses Are Signing Up for Ethics 101" by John A. Byrne (*Business Week,* February 15, 1988, pp. 56-57). Let us quote from two paragraphs on the item: "Hertz Corp. has overcharged consumers and insurers $13 million for repairs to damaged rental cars":

> ...Hertz has an ethics code and requires its employees to sign a compliance statement, but it didn't seem to make a difference.
> ...Senior management approved this practice on the advice of in-house legal counsel, who pointed out that...competitors...followed a similar practice. Unlike the competitors, however, Hertz failed to disclose to customers that they would pay for damages at 'prevailing retail rates.'

Most of the main article, however, refers to the efforts of the leading good-practice companies as described in The Business Roundtable publication presented in our Appendix B-4. The above quotations show that a code of ethics is not a substitute for the capacity to recognize the presence of an ethical dilemma or the will to act accordingly.

Overall Conditions and Trends

In many cases, a change for the better is made more difficult by the impact of various external forces and conditions. Consider the following lines written by the historian Barbara W. Tuchman ("A Nation in Decline?" *The New York Times Magazine,* September 20, 1987, pp. 55-58):

> It does seem that the knowledge of a difference between right and wrong is absent from our society, as if it had floated away in a shadowy night after the last World War. So remote is the concept that even to speak of right or wrong, marks one to the younger generation as old-fashioned, reactionary and out of touch.

Or another quote, from "Building Ethics from the Classroom Up," by Frank G. Goble (*The Wall Street Journal,* January 8, 1988, p. 18):

> People today don't seem to know the difference between right and wrong....Financiers, presidential candidates, corporate executives, even ministers, are criticized severely for their 'unethical' behavior....Business leaders in many communities have urged schools to put more emphasis on character development and have helped raise funds to pay for the programs.

Perhaps we are witnessing just another period of real or perceived changes. The decline notion may be simply the reflection of an increase in the detection rate combined with a greater willingness to expose those events to public scrutiny. It appears that such developments, at least as far as business is involved, come in waves. Then everybody gets busy. Some of the repercussions may have a significant effect.

A little over a decade ago, for example, a major resulting change was the Foreign Corrupt Practices Act, in effect since December 1977. It amended the Securities Exchange Act of 1934. The new Act, moreover, covered all U.S. companies, even nonpublic companies not otherwise covered by the Act of 1934.

This time, more than 10 years later, among the immediate effects are heightened ethical sensitivity in general and recognition that no company can afford to be complacent. More company managements are giving serious attention to the state of ethics in their companies, regardless of the company's relative standing as to the standards of conduct, in principle or in practice.

Chapter 2

Research Purposes and Methods

The First Phase

The research for this project was conducted in two distinct phases, almost exactly two years apart. The work on the first phase, carried out from February 1986 to May 1986, was intended to serve as NAA's contribution to the National Commission on Fraudulent Financial Reporting (the Treadway Commission).

The first-phase report, "Impact of Professionalism and Codes of Corporate Conduct on Financial Reporting," was submitted to the Commission in June 1986. Figure 2 shows the Commission's Abstract of this report, as it appears on p. 101 of the Commission's final report released in October 1987. (See Appendix A-3 for a summary description of the Commission's report.)

The research work of the first phase was consistent with the objectives delineated by the Commission. The subject matter dealt primarily with the Commission's principal concern — fraudulent financial reporting. The Commission viewed the findings and recommendations favorably and discussed them with the researcher at the July 1986 meeting of the Commission.

Figure 3 gives a condensed version of the recommendations contained in the report to the Commission, those that seem pertinent to the purposes of both project phases.

The Second Phase

The NAA also commissioned the second phase of the project, carried out from February 1988 through May 1988.

The in-house documentation collected from major U.S. corporations in the first phase served also in the second phase as the primary reference for company practices. The researcher updated those mate-

Corporate Codes of Conduct

Figure 2

RESEARCH STUDY: Impact of Professionalism and Codes of Corporate Conduct on Financial Reporting

PRIMARY RESEARCHER: Stephen Landekich, Research Executive National Association of Accountants

STUDY SPONSOR: National Association of Accountants

ABSTRACT

This study describes and analyzes two predominant ethical forces that come to bear on the financial reporting process—the corporate ethical climate and professional codes of ethics. With respect to the corporate ethical climate, in-house documentation of ethically related policies and procedures was requested from 103 chief executives of 48 industrial and 55 nonindustrial companies selected randomly from *Fortune* 500 listings. Fifty-one usable responses were received (19 industrial and 32 nonindustrial) from companies headquartered in 20 states and the District of Columbia. The 32 nonindustrial participants included banks (9), utilities (6), retail merchandising (6), transportation (5), insurance (3), and other services (3).

Responses to the request for documentation of ethically related policies and procedures indicated widespread awareness of the effective role that ethical guidance can play in corporate administration. Although the views and policies of the participants differed considerably, the ethical climate did not seem to be correlated with respective management styles. Rather, the basic aim of ethical guidance generally was to achieve a corporate ethical climate consistent with the professed corporate self-image. Areas specifically covered usually were those requiring extra diligence, those offering opportunities for undesirable behavior, those involving ethical dilemmas, or areas where any below-standard actions or attitudes might be especially harmful.

The study also examines professional codes of ethics of the American Institute of Certified Public Accountants (AICPA), the Financial Executives Institute, the Institute of Internal Auditors, and the National Association of Accountants. Both standards of competence and integrity are incorporated into these codes as expressions of professionalism. However, due in part to the absence of strong enforcement clauses in these codes, organizational and situational forces tend to be dominant when on-the-job ethical dilemmas arise. This finding points once again to the critical role that a positive corporate ethical climate plays in enhancing the reliability of the financial reporting process.

Figure 2 (continued)

The study also cautions that while improved accounting and auditing standards may help independent public accountants prevent and detect fraudulent financial reporting, these are not substitutes for a willingness to place professional ethics above the pressures of the accounting marketplace. The AICPA's code of ethics presently endorses several levels of independence to accommodate a variety of services performed by its members. The study suggests that the AICPA consider linking the ethical concept of independence more directly to the auditor's public trust. This linkage may result in a different interpretation of what constitutes undesirable conflicts of interest in the independent public accountant's unique role.

Figure 3
Recommendations to the Commission[1]

• It is recommended that professional examinations and continuing education programs encompass business and professional ethics, including codes of ethics adopted by the closely related professions.
• All representative business and professional groups should jointly organize a nationwide campaign on ethics. Also, a permanent "ethics forum" should be established as a means of inter-organizational consultation and coordination.
• Ethical dilemmas are substantially reduced in a favorable corporate ethical climate. It is recommended that publicly owned enterprises adopt codes of ethics for all employees, officers and members of boards of directors.
• It is the responsibility of corporate management to protect and promote ethical fitness of all employees by removing or restricting undue situational pressures in the on-the-job environment. The areas involving relatively high ethical risks should be covered by special sets of ethical standards, in addition to the companywide code of ethics.
• All codes of ethics should contain adequate provisions on interpretation, compliance, oversight and enforcement. It is preferable to designate/establish specific positions and/or units, such as an ethics committee, which are given the appropriate responsibility/authority.
• Integrity of financial reporting is the responsibility of every employee. Cooperation with internal and external auditors is an ethical requirement to be stated in corporate codes of ethics.
• It is the responsibility of legislative, regulations issuing and standards setting bodies, governmental or private, to give full consideration to the ethical implications and to evaluate the degree of ethical risk caused by the ethical dilemmas related to application and enforcement.

---

[1]Compiled from the Recommendations in the report to the National Commission on Fraudulent Financial Reporting.

rials and expanded the research base with materials from additional companies.

In the second phase of the project, the primary concern was the impact of ethical conduct on company progress and ethics as an essential element in company strength and success, in an overall sense, rather than ethics solely as a means of reducing fraud in financial reporting.

The overall emphasis was on the practicable means and realistic goals. This report is based on the experience of major corporations but is applicable to smaller companies as well.

Management accountants, the traditional "law and order" housekeepers, especially in smaller companies, should understand that a higher level of corporate ethics is their best ally. Their control functions are not intentionally de-emphasized in this study. Consistent maintenance of an adequate sense of ethics throughout a company should facilitate their work and enable them to direct their attention toward the most sensitive or vulnerable areas. Whatever reduces the pervasiveness of indifference or questionable practices narrows the range of unethical acts or makes them more conspicuous and easier to prevent or detect.

Research Design

Initial Research Hypotheses

The design of this study is based on the researcher's hypothesis that the corporate ethical climate, as evidenced in the overall company policies, must be favorable for its code of ethics to be effective. Whether various control systems, including both internal and external auditing, work as planned also depends to an important degree on the environment.

With respect to the corporate ethical climate, this study was designed to find out:

1. Which ethical values and concerns are embedded in the managerial style of major U.S. companies.
2. How the ethical side of company endeavors is expressed in terms of respective policies and procedures.
3. What is being communicated to employees and others.
4. Which instruments monitor observance of the stated policies and procedures.

The researcher established four research hypotheses as to the expected findings:

1. Many large companies have written policies and procedures on the subject of the study.
2. Their willingness to disclose those materials to the researcher would provide a satisfactory level of response and participation.
3. Corporate policies differ in many respects, but the substantive similarities would enable the researcher to identify certain common "core" elements.
4. At least some of the policy differences are attributable to one or more identifiable factors and circumstances.

The research design also was affected by the various inescapable constraints. The inquiry was focused on organizational means rather than their effectiveness. This choice does not assume necessarily that actual corporate dealings are in conformity with the spirit and letter of corporate policies.

Our premise — our basic research hypothesis at that point — was that proper attention to the ethical side of business is a sound and necessary part of company practice. The essence of ethics is that it resides within individual human beings, but ample evidence shows that this personal characteristic can be strengthened, further developed, and made more effective — for the benefit of the corporation as well as the individuals. It is in this sense that we address various constructive means, most already implemented in many companies, that make ethics a valuable company resource.

Methods and Sources

In both phases of the project, the principal research methods were examinations and analyses of:

1. In-house documentation on ethics and related matters, as developed and implemented in major U.S. corporations.
2. Company managements' comments and clarifications.
3. Codes of ethics issued by the leading U.S. and Canadian member organizations of the professionals involved in corporate accounting, financial reporting, and auditing.
4. Annual reports and annual meeting materials of U.S. and foreign companies of various sizes.

5. Relevant literature, including the pertinent coverage in news
media.

Among the supplementary sources were: (1) corporate executives'
descriptions and explanations of the approaches and actions taken
by their companies, as well as their personal reasoning, comments,
and conclusions — specific and general; (2) discussions at two sessions
of the Commission; and (3) consultations with NAA.

The second phase of the project also included: (1) updating of the
company in-house materials, (2) gathering of in-house materials from
additional companies, (3) using a new set of annual reports and
annual meeting materials, (4) updating the literature reviews, and (5)
preparing appendix materials. The change in the central theme resulted
in a relative de-emphasis of fraudulent financial reporting.

Research Sample

Sample Selection

The initial sample of 103 companies was drawn at random from the
listings of *Fortune* 1,000 companies — 500 industrial and 500 nonindustrial. The selected sample was composed of 48 industrial and 55
nonindustrial companies.

In a letter to the chief executive officers of the companies in the
sample, the researcher asked for their cooperation in collecting all
in-house documentation dealing with ethics and related matters,
including instances of upper-level executive fraud.

Response

Written responses were received from 56 companies — a response
rate of 54.4%.

Many responses included unsolicited offers of further active participation and support. The researcher interpreted this responsiveness
as a strong confirmation of the hypothesis that major companies, as
a rule, are fully aware of the significance of ethics and committed to
business conduct at a high level of ethics.

Materials enclosed with the initial responses were voluminous.
Two respondents indicated that their companies had no written policies
on corporate conduct or ethics. Some respondents stressed the con-

fidential nature of the materials, one asked that they subsequently be destroyed, and two wanted them returned.

Updated Sample

Among the responses to the researcher's letter mailed two years later, regarding the updating of the initial materials, several companies sent in the revised or amended versions. Some indicated that no substantial changes were made in the interim period, and one chose not to provide additional information.

The updated sample contains usable in-house materials of 49 companies — 19 industrial and 30 nonindustrial — with corporate headquarters in 20 states and the District of Columbia. The 30 nonindustrial companies include: banks (9), retail merchandising (6), utilities (5), transportation (4), insurance (3), and other services (3).

Letters from the participating companies contained useful information and offered valuable insights regarding company views, practices, and programs. Figure 4 groups respondents by position (title).

Figure 4
Respondents from the Companies

Chairman, Vice Chairman, Executive or Senior Vice President, Treasurer	21
Vice President	18
General or Corporate Controller, General Auditor	5
Director of Corporate Auditing or Accounting	5
Assistant Vice President, Assistant Controller, and other	_7_
Total	56

Additional Evidence

In a separate search for in-house documentation during the second phase of this study, the researcher requested and received materials from 12 companies: 10 industrial and two nonindustrial. Some materials were acquired for reference or illustrative purposes, such as Johnson & Johnson's Credo and Dana Corporation's policies.

Overview of Methods in Ethics Research

Questionnaire Surveys and Data Collection

No mail questionnaire surveys were used in either of the two phases of this study. For our purposes, sufficient factual data, such as codes of ethics and topics they covered, descriptions of numerous programs, and numbers and percentages of organizations, already had been covered elsewhere, before the beginning of our project. For example, a report issued in 1980, *Implementation and Enforcement of Codes of Ethics in Corporations and Associations*, presents the results of a mail survey sponsored by the Ethics Research Center and conducted by Opinion Research Foundation, a subsidiary of Arthur D. Little, Inc. Questionnaires were mailed to the companies that already had a code of ethics. The reported findings refer to 74 companies — 10 participants in the testing phase and 64 respondents.

The files on the companies with codes of ethics were expanded during the period between the first and second phase of our project, particularly by the increasing number and activity of business ethics centers and other organizations. For instance, The Conference Board's Watson Research Collection included 238 corporate codes of conduct by the time the Board's latest survey, *Corporate Ethics*, was undertaken (see Appendix B-1).

Some previous mail surveys centered on questions about various ethical issues or opinions and beliefs. For example, an opinion survey of key business leaders on ethical standards and behavior, *Ethics in American Business* by Touche Ross & Co., presents statistically and graphically as well as analytically the responses to eight questions, ranging from Ethics and Competitiveness to Most and Least Effective Measures for Encouraging Ethical Business Behavior (see Appendix B-3).

Discussions and Case Studies

Other suitable ways for airing controversies are panel discussions and/or conferences. Both may involve case studies to focus the discussion on certain types of ethics situations.

Conferences and panels, prior to a research study, provide the input and/or review the proposed research design. After publication of the study, they provide forums for discussions of the applications and thus also disseminate the research results. Both means were used in The Conference Board research mentioned above.

Much of the support as well as output (publications, conferences, programs) comes from business ethics research centers. Some are independent, but most are associated with universities. The required funding is provided either in the form of sponsorships of individual research projects or by contributions to the centers from business and CPA firms, foundations, and professional/educational organizations. Sixteen centers are listed in *Research in Corporate Social Performance and Policy* (see Appendix C-1).

Research Programs of the Commissions

A major effort, such as the Packard Commission (Appendix A-1 and Appendix A-2) or the Treadway Commission (Appendix A-3), employs a multitude of information sources. The Packard Commission's report includes references to the sources. The Treadway Commission directed an extensive research program, using a variety of research methods. Its significant findings are incorporated into the text of the Commission's report as well as summarized in the appendices.

Descriptive and Normative Approaches

Altogether, there is a wide assortment of research designs and methods. The critical task in research design is to select the most effective method or methods to fit the circumstances.

Some purposes may be served best by well-researched descriptive presentations, as in *Corporate Ethics: A Prime Business Asset* by The Business Roundtable (see Appendix B-4). Such "empirical" research, especially as combined with advanced analytical and interpretive techniques, is gaining more recognition from academic researchers as well.

The "normative" research also contributes insights valuable in practical application, especially if it does not merely elaborate on the ideas explored or the concepts established by the previous researchers. Appendix C contains a variety of approaches used in scholarly research.

Chapter 3

Concepts and Perceptions
of Business Ethics

Business Responsibilities

The ethical side of business often is considered in reference to the powers and responsibilities of businessmen. The underlying question is the role of business in our society.

Manifestations of business power encounter a great deal of opposition. On the other hand, the public demands more activity on the part of business in meeting various social aims and goals.

The basic rationale for the existence of business — its fundamental social responsibility — is to do its best in producing goods and services. This responsibility, however, rarely gets much attention in the context of business ethics discussions.

Thinking of business ethics as a set of standards related to various responsibilities is a useful way of explaining and classifying these standards. Businessmen themselves tend to use this approach when they try to define their ethical standards in terms of responsibilities to the company "constituencies."

Use of the business-responsibilities approach often is intended to stress certain selected worthy causes. The resulting standards become the means of evaluating compliance of business with the requirements or expectations. The emphasis is on the need to be served by business rather than on the underlying ethics. Hence, the responsibility views converge with the power image of business. Only the direction is reversed. The business power is welcome as long as it is exercised in the desired manner.

Social Involvement

The outcome of the responsibility-oriented social-involvement procedure often does not go beyond the self-evident motivations of special-interest advocates. Then the only question that remains is to ascertain how much is enough to qualify a company as being responsive to the demands that have been assigned to it with respect to a particular set of nonmarket responsibilities.

It is in this sense that companies get to be judged primarily in terms of one or another special responsibility or pressure group concern. Company management market performance and responsibilities to company constituencies become almost incidental.

Responsibility vs. Fraud

Companies apparently have learned how to cope with the ever increasing responsibility demands and how to resolve any consequent ethical dilemmas. A serious problem may occur when a company is forced to adopt a pattern of activity that is not in the best interests of its overall performance. Sudden changes in the general direction of outside pressures or a material change in government regulations or in economic conditions also present problems, sometimes of critical importance.

For example, the current revelations of the horrendous cumulative losses of savings and loan institutions are disclosing some of the consequences of an adverse confluence of events. In some cases, the situation got even worse due to various ill-advised efforts to rectify the problems. The ethical damage of such a mass failure and subsequent bailout can be enormous.

Many of the failures by savings and loan institutions can be traced directly to the losses caused by unethical acts and practices. Financial fraud, however, is not restricted to savings and loan institutions.

Figure 5 shows the trend of financial fraud in the nation's banks. It was reproduced from Charles McCoy's article "Financial Fraud: Theories Behind Nationwide Surge in Bank Swindles" (*The Wall Street Journal*, October 2, 1987, p. 23). The author refers to various theories offered by "prosecutors, regulators and investigators...Some are predictable, some novel. But they all begin at the same point: GREED."

Social Impact

Areas of Social Impact - The NAA Taxonomy

"Corporate activities have social as well as economic impacts." This is the first line in the Report of the NAA Committee on Accounting for Corporate Social Performance (*Management Accounting*, February 1974, pp. 39-41). The Committee drafted a taxonomy on Areas of Corporate Social Performance. The draft was tested in a company survey conducted by this researcher.

Figure 5

An Epidemic of Scams and Embezzlements
Annual losses from fraud in U.S.
(In millions of dollars)

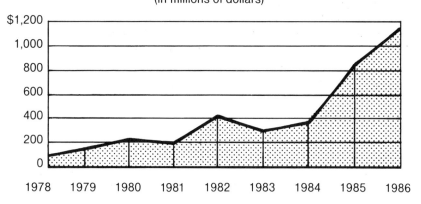

'At rock bottom, the real culprit is old-fashioned, pure, unadulterated, materialistic, gimme-gimme greed,' says a trial lawyer in the Justice Department's fraud division.

Source: Federal Bureau of Investigation

Figure 6 presents a major portion of the final text of the taxonomy as it appeared in the published Committee Report.

The objective of the Committee was to develop systems of accounting for corporate social performance. One important purpose was to educate and motivate managers to think through the social consequences of all decisions. The NAA's research studies and published research reports supplemented the effort of the Committee. These studies covered all major areas other than community involvement, because that subject already had been sufficiently researched.

Figure 7 shows typical examples of social performance for each of the four major areas: community involvement, human resources, physical resources and environmental contributions, and product or service contributions. The list also appeared in the published Committee Report.

Figure 6
Areas of Corporate Social Performance

I. Introduction

Corporate activities have social as well as economic impacts. For example, economic activities are measured by financial accounting procedures and are reported in financial statements. There are established standards for this. There are, however, no established standards for measuring and reporting corporate social performance.

Social performance reflects the impact of a corporation's activities upon society. This embodies the performance of its economic functions and other actions taken to contribute to the quality of life. These activities may extend beyond meeting the letter of the law, the pressures of competition or the requirements of contracts.

II. Relevance of Profitability to Corporate Social Performance

[One paragraph omitted]

In this respect, profits are fundamental. Perpetuation of a private sector corporation and its potential for continued social contributions depends upon a satisfactory degree of profitability. Thus, net income is basically a short-run assessment of wealth creation which has social significance. Resources provided by this net income may be variously distributed thus providing various amounts of social product, but a profitable organization necessarily provides satisfaction for its many constituencies.

While relationships between economic and social phenomena are complicated, they are in many aspects complementary, and it would be a serious mistake to assume otherwise. Until these relationships are understood better it appears reasonable to pursue the subject of corporate social performance measurement by dealing with an expanded set of performance categories that build onto the present economic-based measures familiar to accountants and business managers.

III. Recognizing Corporate Social Performance [Omitted]
IV. Major Areas of Social Performance

Social performance may be considered under the following four major areas (in alphabetical order):

A. Community involvement
B. Human resources
C. Physical resources and environmental contributions
D. Product or service contributions

Community involvement includes those socially oriented activities which tend primarily to benefit the general public. "Community" in this sense denotes

Figure 6 (continued)

more than the specific geographic area in which the corporation has plants and offices.

Human resources is an internal area. It covers that social performance which is directed to the well-being of employees.

Physical resources and environmental contributions include those activities which are directed toward alleviating or preventing environmental deterioration. Again, these relate to more than the geographical location of corporate facilities. An example would be a product which is inherently polluting and thus would have adverse environmental effects wheresoever it was used.

Product or service contributions of a social nature deal with relations with customers, or effects on society accruing or arising from products or services. They reflect the concerns of a corporation for generating and maintaining customer satisfaction over and above that of a "caveat emptor" attitude.

These four major areas of social performance are neither exhaustive nor mutually exclusive. For example, a decision as to a plant location would certainly give consideration to community involvement, environmental contributions and human resources. They are intended to encourage uniformity in appraising social performance.

The following list of items under each of the four major areas identifies typical examples of social performance. The lists are not intended to be all inclusive. Neither are the items listed in any sequence of importance. Comments following each item are for explanation [see Figure 7].

Source: *Management Accounting,* February 1974, p. 40.

Figure 7

Typical Examples of Social Performance

A. COMMUNITY INVOLVEMENT

1. General philanthropy—Corporate support of educational institutions, cultural activities, recreational programs, health and community welfare agencies and similar eleemosynary organizations
2. Public and private transportation—Alleviating or preventing urban transportation problems, including the provision of mass transportation of employees
3. Health services—Providing health care facilities and services and the support programs to reduce disease and illness
4. Housing—Improving the standard of dwellings, the construction of needed dwellings and the financing of housing renovation and construction
5. Aid in personal and business problems—Alleviation of problems related to the physically handicapped, child care, minority businesses, disadvantaged persons, etc.

Figure 7 (continued)

6. Community planning and improvement—Programs of urban planning and renewal, crime prevention, etc.
7. Volunteer activities—Encouraging and providing time for employees to be active as volunteers in community activities
8. Specialized food programs—The provision of meals to meet the dietary needs of the aged, the infirm, the disadvantaged child and other groups
9. Education—The development and implementation of educational programs to supplement those of the public or private schools such as work study programs; and employee service on school boards, school authorities and college university trustee and advisory boards

B. HUMAN RESOURCES

1. Employment practices—Providing equal job opportunities for all persons, creation of summer job opportunities for students, and recruiting in depressed areas
2. Training programs—Providing programs for all employees to increase their skills, earning potential and job satisfaction
3. Promotion policies—Recognizing the abilities of all employees and providing equal opportunities for promotion
4. Employment continuity—Scheduling production so as to minimize lay-offs and recalls, maintaining facilities in efficient operating condition so that they will not have to be abandoned because of deterioration, and exploring all feasible alternatives to closing a facility
5. Remuneration—Maintaining a level of total salaries and wages plus benefits which is in line with others in either the industry or community
6. Working conditions—Providing safe, healthful and pleasant working environment
7. Drugs and alcohol—Providing education and counseling for employees to prevent or alleviate problems in these and similar areas
8. Job enrichment—Providing the most meaningful work experiences practical for all employees
9. Communications—Establishing and maintaining two-way communication between all levels of employees to secure suggestions, to provide information as to what the company is actually doing and how each department's activities relate to the total corporate activity, and to inform employees' families and friends of corporate activities

C. PHYSICAL RESOURCES AND ENVIRONMENTAL CONTRIBUTIONS

1. Air—Timely meeting of the law and going beyond the law in avoiding the creation of, alleviating, or eliminating pollutants in these areas
2. Water—Timely meeting of the law and going beyond the law in avoiding the creation of, alleviating, or eliminating pollutants in these areas

Figure 7 (continued)

3. Sound—Timely meeting of the law and going beyond the law in avoiding the creation of, alleviating, or eliminating pollutants in these areas
4. Solid waste-Disposal of solid waste in such a manner as to minimize contamination, reduce its bulk, etc., and the design of processes and products which will minimize the creation of solid waste
5. Use of scarce resources—The conservation of existing energy sources, the development of new energy sources, and the conservation of scarce materials
6. Aesthetics—The design and location of facilities in conformance with surroundings and with pleasing architecture and landscaping

D. PRODUCT OR SERVICE CONTRIBUTIONS

1. Completeness and clarity of labeling, packaging, and marketing representation—Assurance that labeling and representation as to methods of use, limitations on use, hazards of use, shelf-life, quantity of contents, and quality cannot be misunderstood
2. Warranty provisions—Adherence to all stated or implied warranties of a product with implementation through timely recalls, repairs or replacements
3. Responsiveness to consumer complaints—Prompt and complete responses to all complaints received
4. Consumer education—Literature and media programs to keep consumers informed of product or service characteristics, methods and areas of use of products, and of planned product changes or discontinuances
5. Product quality—Assurance through adequate control—"quality assurance" —that quality is at least equal to what customers may reasonably expect on the basis of company representations
6. Product safety—Design or formulation and packaging of products to minimize possibilities of harm or injury in product use
7. Content and frequency of advertising—Giving full consideration to the omission of any media material which may be adverse or offensive; and the avoidance of repetition to the extent that it becomes repugnant
8. Constructive research—Orienting technical and market research to meet defined social needs and to avoid creating social and environmental problems or to minimize such problems; e.g., energy consumption

Source: *Management Accounting*, February 1974, p. 41.

Advantages of Corporate Social Involvement

Incentives for Corporate Programs

The idea of accounting measurement systems, as envisaged by the NAA Committee on Accounting for Corporate Social Performance, has not been pursued. This does not mean necessarily that companies have not been experimenting in developing and using various means of measuring the social impact of their activities.

Many companies have established new managerial decision-making criteria so as to achieve a more desirable social impact. It also is true that some company programs aiming at higher-level managerial attitudes and practices would not have been considered if other methods, not requiring managerial reforms or retraining, had been successful.

Efforts in Practice: Examples

Take, for example, the case of General Motors. It was not until very recently that "the world's largest bureaucracy" decided that the time had come to become more sensitive to "people power." Both expressions given in quotes above are taken from a report by two staff reporters of *The Wall Street Journal,* Jacob M. Schlesinger and Paul Ingrassia, as published on pp. A1 and A6 of the January 12, 1989, issue of the *Journal:*

> But the humanization of General Motors really involves persuading managers to accept ideas and challenges from their subordinates — and convincing the subordinates they really mean it. For a notoriously hierarchical company, that demands that the most crucial change come at the top, from Mr. Smith. [GM Chairman]

Elsewhere in this long report, the authors quote GM's Executive Vice President, Alan Smith, "a financial man long considered the quintessential humorless bean-counter: 'People, not fixed assets or technology, are what really make the difference in the bottom line.'"

The reporters also are aware of other aspects or possible further twists, as well as of some less advertised reasons for the apparent willingness of the rank and file to overlook, for the time being, the possibility that most of those changes are not more than "cosmetic gestures." For example:

> ...But, in fact, a major motivation isn't necessarily a new sense of self-worth, it's pure fear. More than 40,000 GM workers are currently on layoff, and all 310,000 active plant workers are acutely aware of that...
>
> All concede that GM's cultural-form effort remains fragile.

In this context, let us move on to another of the many recent media stories. This one is about Procter & Gamble's move to boost the percentage of shares under the control of its employee stock ownership plan (ESOP). It is hardly coincidental that this action comes at the time when ESOPs appear to be effective as a takeover defense — an important current concern of P&G top management. Some observers think, however, that the main goal was to get the significant tax breaks available under such plans.

For the purposes of our example, it does not really matter whether one or the other or both of those reasons caused the action. Our purpose here is to illustrate the interlocking effects of a host of factors and events that may be at work whenever we witness a major new trend in company practices. The concluding observations in those stories (articles) are rather skeptical regarding the power of ethics and related notions to attract on their own merits a widespread loyal following of company executives.

Conscience Awards

To conclude this section, let us mention a noteworthy effort to extend public recognition for company accomplishments related to certain areas of social impact. The Council on Economic Priorities, a nonprofit research organization, awards its annual America's Corporate Conscience Awards for the work in the areas identified by the Council. Among the award categories are: community action, charitable giving, most improved corporate disclosure, and animal rights. The Council's awards in 1989 were given for exemplary performance in several categories, such as a tree-planting program in Guatemala and support of small businesses owned by women, minorities, and the handicapped.

A pocket guide issued by the Council on Economic Priorities, "Shopping for a Better World," is used by an increasing number of consumers, according to various news media releases. On the other hand, at least some of the companies accused of lacking a sense of social responsibility maintain that they simply do not want to support that kind of social monitoring. Either way, informed observers tend to agree that it is difficult to gauge how corporate social behavior ratings affect sales volume of their products.

Use and Abuse of Business Power

The "Proper Role" Question

An article by Michael Kinsley, "Companies as Citizens: Should They Have a Conscience?" (*The Wall Street Journal*, February 19,

1987, p. 29), contains his comments on two books, both of which accuse business of lacking "responsibility." His general remarks include the following:

> ...The proper social role of the corporation is to produce the best peanut butter at the lowest price, leaving to individuals and to the political system such matters as support for the arts and how much we spend on defense. There's a lot to be said, even from a left-wing viewpoint, for the idea that corporations should keep to their own sphere and not attempt to become all-embracing social-service agencies.
>
> In particular, I am not impressed by corporate charity and cultural benefaction, which amount to executives playing Medici with other people's money...There is a Catch-22 logic behind corporate charity...It's good for the corporate image..., therefore corporate charity is a justifiable expenditure of shareholders' money. But if it's actually a hard-nosed business decision, why give the corporation credit for generosity? In which case the syllogism unravels.

In many ways, prudent exercise of corporate powers is coincidental with sound business decision making. A good constructive relationship with the local community and state is in the interest of both sides. Many states recognize multiple advantages (employment, taxes, and so on) of having a company located there, and they often make special efforts to attract companies to move to their territories. It is fair to assume that a company known for its high ethical standards would be considered particularly attractive.

Involvement in Politics

The use of business powers for political purposes is a very sensitive and delicate area full of ethical dilemmas. In a political power structure in which various special-interest groups wield considerable influence, it appears both warranted and necessary for business as a whole or for an industry or individual company to be active in the political process. As a matter of fact, the interests within business are so diverse that not infrequently companies or industries take opposite positions on a question under consideration. Even on subjects involving common principles, such as free competition, some companies do not support deregulation. Actually, very few issues — lower tax rates is one — have the support of the whole "business community."

Unfortunately, sometimes a questionable practice is so widespread that it becomes a commonly followed way of doing business. Take, as an example, Joyce Purnick's report, "Campaign Contributors: Seeking to Give or to Receive?" (*The New York Times,* April 1, 1988, pp. B1 & B6):

> For two days, a glittery roster of developers, the newest category of New York City celebrity, testified before the State Commission on Government Integrity to explain, under oath, why they give money to public officials...Some testified that they contributed on the advice of their public relations consultant, and still others said they were afraid of retaliation if they did not make contributions.
>
> ...'If they didn't give, it wouldn't make any difference,' suggests Andrew Cuomo, the Governor's son. 'But they don't know that.'

Chapter 4

Business Ethics
as Seen by Corporations

Corporate Cultures

Symbolic expressions, trappings, and rituals that highlight the real or fictitious self-image of a company can have a profound "magical" impact on employee loyalty and pride, even when originally designed to serve as public relations or product promotion devices. Those phenomena are referred to metaphorically as "corporate cultures." They have been developed over the years by many major well-established companies. The form or extent varies — from a brief slogan to an elaborate program.

Corporate culture is evident in many ways. It usually is identified formally in a written statement of corporate vision or corporate mission or as a set of basic corporate qualities, values, beliefs, or commitments.

The sense of uniqueness sometimes permeates the company policies, activities, and behavioral patterns. In other cases, the main role is to provide a frame of reference and a point of departure for the establishment of detailed statements, policies, and procedures.

Ethical Impact

A strong sense of attachment, loyalty, and responsibility associated with the existence of a particular corporate culture contains an intrinsically ethical element. Corporate culture raises the overall sense of ethical behavior in a convenient, often attractive, way, which is easy to understand and accept.

The question is whether corporate culture is effective as a surrogate means of setting corporate standards of conduct. It seems that a distinct corporate culture incorporates, explicitly or implicitly, a substantial part of corporate ethics. Still, it is not likely that a corporate culture presents a sufficient substitute for a set of standards of conduct. The latter serves at least two additional purposes: to identify ethical dilemmas and to clarify the proper ways of resolving them.

Business vs. Personal Behavior

There is no particular reason to expect any distinct difference between business and personal ethics at the very top of the corporate hierarchy. Identical or very similar ethical dilemmas probably are resolved in the same manner under the same or similar circumstances. In other words, business ethics is best defined by the nature of ethical dilemmas and the ways of resolving them under the conditions and circumstances prevailing in business. Even in identical ethical dilemmas, a business ethics approach requires that some considerations be taken into account that may not be relevant to the resolution of nonbusiness personal dilemmas.

If a company is dominated by a strong CEO or a strong corporate culture it is likely that some differences between business and personal ethics will be introduced, regardless of any distinctions due solely to the differences between ethical dilemmas at the workplace and those in private personal life.

In companies with specific standards of conduct, which reflect a form of ethical consensus, less of a behavioral adjustment will be needed, perhaps none at all. Such standards of conduct appear superior to the "corporate culture" resolutions of ethical dilemmas. Many of those cultures unduly emphasize readily observable behavior, though they call for "the highest ethical principles." Nothing less is good enough. At the same time, the corporate-culture messages leave many of the ethics questions undefined.

Ethics is a personal matter, after all. Corporations cannot act, ethically or otherwise, except through the persons representing them. One might say, therefore, that no business ethics exists separately from personal ethics. Still, the concept of business ethics is meaningful, for it denotes the ethical dilemmas peculiar to business endeavors and the levels of ethics at which such dilemmas commonly are treated and resolved in business.

A company's encouragement and active support of a high level of ethical conduct by its employees edges them toward doing their best. An explicitly stated company position regarding suitable standards of conduct, often issued as a code of ethics, is a powerful means toward gaining still more valuable human resources and attaining an even higher general image and reputation.

The crucial factor is the CEO's awareness of ethics and determination to support it. By its very nature, ethics is indivisible — within a person or company. It is essential, therefore, that the same ethical standards be applicable to all.

Standards of Company Conduct

Managements of some companies in our survey sample hold the view that their companies need not be concerned about ethics to a degree that would require a set of written standards. Such a view was expressed only by a small minority, but it reflects a firm position of their companies. To them, ethics is not an issue that needs a decision or calls for any formal action.

While such views are not shared by most companies in the research sample, it seems appropriate to keep in mind the large-company composition of the sample. A different sample composed of smaller companies might have contained a higher proportion of similar views and positions.

Three Examples

Several types of reasoning underlie these views. Examples given below are selected from the project correspondence file:

1. As a company with a very well-known name, with products sold under that name, there has never been the slightest temptation to deal in a way that would or could tarnish the image of the company. In view of our internal experience, the company has never found it necessary to publish any internal material on a standard of ethics.
2. At the present time we do not have a published statement as to ethical business practices. In our particular case, we have found that this issue is best handled periodically at our regular management meetings. This gives top executives an opportunity to have a dialogue with the management level staff and, as a result, any potential misunderstandings would be clearly eliminated or dealt with at the time.
3. I doubt that dishonesty in the corporate area is any greater or less prevalent than in any other segment of our society. A number of people are crooks, a larger number misconceive or don't understand the directions. Many people and businesses play in games where the rules are (more or less) clear, but where, either only apparently or in fact, those rules are unrealistic or are not applied in an even handed

way, perhaps not applied at all. Enacting a rule without a will to enforce it or if it can't be enforced because it costs too much to do so, possibly was fraudulently conceived.

Dormant Observance of Standards

The above examples show that views and practices of large companies may vary substantially with respect to an important aspect of company operations and management responsibilities. It is not plausible that conditions in their companies differ that much.

At a closer look, on the other hand, company performances vary over the years. This is particularly true of the company referred to in the first example. Statistical data show stagnant sales (revenues) both in total and per-share amounts over the last decade, ending in 1988. The earnings per share show a steady decline over the same period, while the net worth is lower than 10 years ago.

All this is not conclusive evidence, by any means, that their complacent attitude toward ethics is a reflection of their general managerial style, characterized by the apparent lack of initiative and success. The researcher has not explored company managerial style in any detail, but a tentative conclusion can be drawn from this and other cases that managerial style does not, as a rule, have much impact on the attitudes toward standards of ethics.

A meaningfully different picture arises, however, when one attempts to reach beyond the professed views on standards of ethics. Then we see some companies with carefully manicured ethical landscapes whose actual role does not go any further than the role of the beautiful lawns surrounding their headquarter compounds. Those are the companies with "dormant observance of standards" that probably should be the prime targets of any effort to raise the level of ethics in our large companies, for two reasons:

1. The codes of ethics that are not meant to be enforced, in whole or in large part, may cause significant damage to the company's ethical climate.
2. The lack of attention to and tolerance of violations reinforces a widespread notion that corporate codes of ethics are either a form of public relations "window dressing" or do not make any significant difference.

The companies falling into the dormant standards category within the research sample are not an exception as is the aforementioned company that has no standards of ethics. The dormant-standards companies constitute about one-fourth of the sample, according to the researcher's rather tentative classification. This finding is somewhat consistent with the caustic remarks about game playing, declared in the third example above.

An Illustration

Some companies, especially defense contractors, have recently displayed sudden eagerness to adopt stringent standards of ethics. On the face of it, the policy changes are not very convincing despite (or because of) wide publicity orchestrated by the respective companies. Let us illustrate both the skepticism and the recognition in one single case:

> *Corruption thwarter*
> Stanley Pace, 64, knows all about ethics. He...was recently appointed chairman of General Dynamics...the embattled defense contractor....
> ...On January 16 he turned up before the National Press Club in Washington to lay out the changes.
> ...'Aren't you simply promising to be honest?' and 'Is this what it takes to make a corporation honest?' Questions continued in this vein for half an hour.... It would seem Pace will have an uphill battle proving his campaign is more than cosmetic. (By Janet Fix in *Forbes*, February 10, 1986, p. 140.)

Less than one month later, in *The New York Times* of March 6, 1986, Nicholas D. Kristoff in his "Gentle Persuasion at General Dynamics," said:

> For now, Mr. Pace is trying to make changes in an area that he, and the public, has become all too familiar with — business ethics at General Dynamics. ...And there seems to be a greater sensitivity to ethical questions. Two weeks ago, for example, a young worker in San Diego, who said his boss ordered him to falsify a time card, protested the practice. In the past, he had silently assented. This time, a meeting was hurriedly held, at which the manager denied the charge. The confrontation ended in a stalemate, but workers, who felt the protesting employee triumphed, say the manager will probably not make any future suggestions about time cards.

The illustration above appears to have shed light on a subtle but crucial interaction between the events at the top and their repercussions throughout the company. A firm ethical posture of a determined and outspoken CEO inevitably lifts the level of the corporate ethical climate, even if the policy originated as a response to outside pressures. Similarly, an ethical conversion of an authoritarian CEO works even faster than the educational ethics programs do.

One should not be tempted to make too much of a single occurrence in one company. On the other hand, the apparent preponderance of "cosmetic" ethics reforms makes it easy to remain skeptical, although the illustration does offer evidence of cause and effect in a field of inquiry where hard evidence is not readily available.

Nor should one overlook some questions that have remained open, such as: Why did no other employees offer any corroborating material from their own experiences with the same manager? One may assume that he behaved similarly on other occasions and with other workers under his supervision. Nor is it known what, if anything, happened subsequently — whether the triumphant employee was given the opportunity to regret his refusal to play the game.

The events associated with the questions raised above, as well as many other questions of this type, are very important and often decisive regarding the state of the corporate ethical climate. They are at least as educational as are many of the cases concocted for the demonstrations within various ethics programs. The events are real, and unless strong managerial resistance to change prevents, their effects are sustainable. The impact of promotional ethics shows does not necessarily survive the active phase of the related programs. Without further reinvigorating action or program, any favorable effect gradually lapses into dormant observance.

In this context, it is encouraging to learn of many companies that quite recently have adopted codes of ethics or other ethics-related policies. Perhaps even more noteworthy is the evidence showing that the companies that adopted their codes of ethics some years ago are trying continually to make them still more effective.

Constructive Developments

Let us again illustrate three types of further developments with examples from the latest company executive responses (1988) to the researcher's inquiry:

1. The company has extensively broadened its efforts, with a sharper focus on the key ethical questions. A new two-volume Business Conduct Guidelines was issued and a new training device has been developed (a one-hour video tape with accompanying course booklet).
2. Statement of Policy has been revised somewhat in response to suggestions of the Treadway Commission. Additionally, the Statement's acknowledgment form has been revised to require responses

to specific questions in order to provide a more direct relationship to business conduct guidelines prescribed by the Statement of Policy.
3. The earlier policies and their implementation remain in place. We have no changes (since 1986) to report. Behind these policies and procedures is a broader framework of Company values that we seek to foster on an ongoing basis. We are committed to ensuring that these values remain a vital part of our corporate culture, and we are convinced that an explicit commitment to these general principles reinforces employee adherence to standards in particular areas such as accounting.

In this connection, we are in the process of reviewing and upgrading, where necessary, our communication and training efforts related to business ethics and basic Company values. This does not, however, involve new policies or programs, but rather an augmenting of existing efforts.

It is clear that corporate managements recognize the value of a good company and business reputation. Not all of them, however, are equally cognizant of its foundation — corporate ethics.

Meaning and Attributes of Corporate Ethics

Basic Ingredients and Dimensions

No single item in the collection of statements presented in Figure 8 has been formulated to serve as a definition of business ethics.

The concept of business ethics is rendered here as an outline or, rather, those statements offer a rough approximation of the multiple dimensions of ethics as viewed from different angles or directions. Taken together, the statements are descriptive of business ethics as seen, experienced, and practiced by corporations. It is probably a multifaceted mirror of the various features of corporate life as well as a portrayal of what they mean by applying the term ethics to corporate behavior.

Instead of or in addition to the concise announcements of company notions of what is basic in corporate ethics, many companies find it useful to give an overview of their general statements. The main ethics or corporate culture documents often have introductory sections in which companies outline their "overriding principles" or present a set of such basic tenets under similar headings.

The statements covered here are spelled out in more detail than the preceding statements so they are considerably longer. Hence, it is not feasible to show more than a few of them, which appear in a condensed format in Figures 9 to 11.

Figure 8

Basic Dimensions of Corporate Ethics

• Corporate integrity is the sum total of the personal integrity of each of our employees around the world. It takes years to build our reputation as a company known for its integrity, but one simple act of an employee can go a long way to destroy it.

• Our most basic ethical standard is to show respect for those whose lives we affect and to treat them as we would expect them to treat us if our positions were reversed.

• There are four fundamental cornerstones: (a) Honesty and candor in all our activities, (b) Fairness in all our dealings, (c) Avoidance of conflicts of interest, and (d) Integrity in our use of corporate resources.

• Simply stated, we must not only be right, we must also look right. The fact that others are engaging in similar conduct does not necessarily make it right for the company.

• Our lack of progress to date is primarily attributable to a widespread perception that upper management has the attitude of, "Do as I say, not as I do." ...First and foremost, we each must think through and change our own behavior. A good indicator...is how much we have changed in our use of power and privilege.

Figure 9

Guidelines

A business enterprise is usually thought of in economic terms. But it is more realistically, and more importantly, an institution of people. These are the overriding principles which must guide us in our conduct as representatives of the Company:

• No "code of conduct" can spell out the appropriate conduct and behavior for every situation with which we will be confronted. In the last analysis we must rely on our own good judgment. Whenever we find ourselves with a hard decision to make, we must seek counsel— either from our colleagues, from our management, the Corporate Ethics Committee, and most importantly, our own conscience.

• One of the most important tenets of our policy is openness. Every transaction we engage in must be correctly recorded.

• We see no conflict between attention to profit and attention to ethics. In fact, the two should go hand in hand. We will prosper most in an environment that is fair, open and morally secure; and as we contribute to such an environment we will also contribute to the good health of the company.

Figure 10

Principles

Service. We shall preserve the company's proud heritage of service with the recognition that building on that tradition is a responsibility we all share equally.

Financial Responsibility. We shall strive constantly to maintain a position of financial strength that enables us to meet the expectations of our shareowners, employees and customers.

Integrity. We shall conduct ourselves so as to honor the finest traditions of our past and maintain the highest possible standards for those who follow us.

People. We are firmly committed to assuring quality work experiences and equal opportunity for our employees, recognizing that the company's success ultimately depends on the performance, teamwork, and spirit of its people.

Progress. We shall recognize our responsibilities as leaders in technological advancement and commit ourselves to the development and implementation of continuing improvements that will be of genuine service to our customers.

Citizenship. We shall accept our responsibilities as individual and corporate citizens of the communities we serve and seek constantly, in our own way, to improve the quality of life for our families and fellow citizens.

Figure 11

Corporate Mission

• Our primary enterprise objective is to increase the value of our shareowners' investment by serving our customers better than and more efficiently than our competitors.

• We will grow in markets where we can create enough advantage to earn a good return for our shareowners. We will redeploy resources from markets where we cannot.

• By achieving our objective, we expect to reward our shareowners, whose continuing investment in the Company is vital, and to reward our employees, whose creativity and commitment to winning through teamwork are the keys to our competitiveness.

Chapter 5

Main Types of Ethics Policy Statements

General Corporate Statements

In some companies, the ethics policy is contained in the statements of corporate policies, along with other policies or as part of them. Most often, ethics is built into the company policies on internal auditing or on conflicts of interest. The relative emphasis and extent or specificity regarding a particular subject usually are related to the industry characteristics, company size, and external circumstances.

Corporate policy statements often bear clear marks of the concerns and pressures that were influential when the company decided to issue such a statement in the first place. Various laws and regulations are covered regularly in those general statements, for example, the Foreign Corrupt Practices Act, policies on affirmative action program/ equal employment opportunity, and antitrust and securities regulations.

Minor references to ethics very often appear within various other specific policies. On the other hand, those ethics-related aspects of other policies may be found within the policy on ethics in many companies.

Internal auditing is an exception. It almost always is covered by a separate policy, though some references to internal and external auditing frequently are included in the ethics policy as well. The same applies, but less frequently, to accounting controls and/or financial records and reports.

A Comprehensive Statement: Dana Policies

Figure 12 shows a self-contained document. As a corporate statement of policies, it speaks for itself. It covers the following topics: earnings, growth, people, planning, organization, customers, communication, and citizenship.

43

All are accommodated on one single page. About one-third of the text deals with a single topic: people. The ethical side of business is accentuated throughout the statement, but one sentence only addresses ethics explicitly: "All Dana people are expected to do business in a professional and ethical manner with integrity."

The reverse side of the sheet is designed so the sheet can be folded. When folded, it becomes a convenient pocket-size leaflet, apparently meant to be carried for easy and frequent reference.

The company has an accompanying promotional piece, "The Direction of Dana," which contains five basic items but no direct reference to the comprehensive policy statement.

This illustration also may serve as an example of the company use of the "corporate culture." It apparently is referred to as "the Dana Style" or "the Dana Management Style," and the expression "Dana people" appears frequently. It is made abundantly clear that this is a company of superior quality and high aspirations which are described and explained, along with the corresponding requirements and expectations.

Figure 12

POLICIES

EARNINGS
The purpose of the Dana Corporation is to earn money for its shareholders and to increase the value of their investment. We believe the best way to do this is to earn an acceptable return by properly utilizing our assets and controlling our cash.
GROWTH
We believe in steady growth to protect our assets against inflation.
We will grow in our selected markets by implementing our market strategies.
PEOPLE
We are dedicated to the belief that our people are our most important asset. Wherever possible, we encourage all Dana people within the entire world organization to become shareholders, or by some other means, own a part of their company.
We believe people respond to recognition, freedom to participate, and the opportunity to develop.
We believe that people should be involved in setting their own goals and judging their own performance. The people who know best how the job should be done are the ones doing it.

Figure 12 (continued)

We believe Dana people should accept only total quality in all tasks they perform.

We endorse productivity plans which allow people to share in the rewards of productivity gains.

We believe that all Dana people should identify with the company. This identity should carry on after they have left active employment.

We believe facilities with people who have demonstrated a commitment to Dana will be competitive and thus warrant our support.

We believe that wages and benefits are the concern and responsibility of managers. The Management Resource Program is a worldwide matter—it is a tool that should be used in the development of qualified Dana people. We encourage income protection, health programs, and education.

We believe that on-the-job training is an effective method of learning. A Dana manager must prove proficiency in at least one line of our company's work—marketing, engineering, manufacturing, financial services, etc. Additionally, these people must prove their ability as supervisors and be able to get work done through other people. We recognize the importance of gaining experience both internationally and domestically.

We believe our people should move across product, discipline and organizational lines. These moves should not conflict with operating efficiency.

We believe in promoting from within. Dana people interested in other positions are encouraged to discuss job opportunities with their supervisor.

Managers are responsible for the selection, education and training of all people.

All Dana people should have their job performance reviewed at least once a year by their supervisors.

We believe in providing programs to support the Dana Style. We encourage professional and personal development of all Dana people.

PLANNING

We believe in planning at all levels.

The Policy Committee is responsible for developing the corporate strategic plan.

Each operating unit within its regional organization is responsible for a detailed five-year business plan. These business plans must support the corporate strategic plan and market strategies. These plans are reviewed annually.

Commitment is a key element of the Dana Management Style. This commitment and performance will be reviewed on a monthly basis by the appropriate regional operating committee and on a semi-annual basis during Mid-Year Reviews.

ORGANIZATION

We discourage conformity, uniformity and centralization.

We believe in a minimum number of management levels. Responsibility should be pushed as far into the organization as possible.

Figure 12 (continued)

Organizational structure must not conflict with doing what is best for all of Dana.

We believe in an organizational structure that allows the individual maximum freedom to perform and participate. This will stimulate initiative, innovation, and the entrepreneurial spirit that is the cornerstone of our success.

We believe in small, highly effective, support groups to service specialized needs of the Policy Committee and the world organization at large as requested. We believe in task forces rather than permanent staff functions.

We do not believe in company-wide procedures. If an organization requires procedures, it is the responsibility of the manager to create them.

CUSTOMERS

Dana is a global company focused on markets and customers. We compete globally by supplying products and services to meet the needs of our customers in our selected markets.

We believe it is absolutely necessary to anticipate our customers' needs for products and services of the highest quality. Once a commitment is made to a customer, every effort must be made to fulfill that obligation.

It is highly desirable to outsource a portion of our production needs. Outsourcing increases our competitiveness and protects the stability of employment for our people. It also protects our assets and assures performance to our customers.

Dana people throughout the organization are expected to know our customers and their needs.

COMMUNICATION

We will communicate regularly with shareholders, customers, Dana people, general public, and financial communities.

It is the job of all managers to keep Dana people informed. Each manager must decide on the best method of communication. We believe direct communication with all of our people eliminates the need for a third party involvement. All managers shall periodically inform their people about the performance and plans of their operation.

CITIZENSHIP

The Dana Corporation will be a good citizen worldwide. All Dana people are expected to do business in a professional and ethical manner with integrity.

Laws and regulations have become increasingly complex. The laws of propriety always govern. The General Counsel and each General Manager can give guidance when in doubt about appropriate conduct. It is expected that no one would willfully violate the law and subject themselves to disciplinary action.

We encourage active participation of all of our people in community action.

We will support worthwhile community causes consistent with their importance to the good of Dana people in the community.

Approved by The Board of Directors   The Policy Committee
Dana Corporation   Dana Corporation

10/28/69   Rev. 12-1-87

Responsibility/Commitment Statements

Responsibilities vs. Commitments

General policy statements often address the main corporate constituencies. The statements sometimes are expressed in terms of the respective responsibilities. The corresponding commitments are stated or implied.

Other companies present their general policy statements as sets of commitments. The corresponding responsibilities are stated or implied.

The commitment approach appears stronger and more impressive — an immediate activity-oriented document. The responsibility approach, on the other hand, appears to be reinforcing the principles already in effect, implying a favorable record of accomplishments.

For a closer look at the two approaches, we have chosen to show three illustrations, the venerable Johnson & Johnson's Credo and responsibility/commitment sets of two other major companies. (Unless the company's identification cannot be avoided, we consistently preserve company anonymity.) The choice highlights the differences between the two approaches both as to form and intended role.

Johnson & Johnson: Our Credo

The J&J's Credo is set as a self-standing and self-contained document, ready to be put into a frame and displayed. Judging by its content, it appears that "Our Credo" can be viewed, in the first place, as a responsibility/commitment general statement, though it serves the purposes of a code of ethics equally well. As Professor Nash writes in her report (see Appendix B-4), "If any business ethics code could be said to have obtained celebrity status in America, it would be the Johnson & Johnson Credo." "Our Credo" is reproduced in Figure 13.

A Commitment Statement

One company's commitment statement is part of its booklet on Standards of Business Ethics and Conduct. The commitment statement precedes a section titled "Responsibilities," which is followed by the main section, "Standards."

This commitment statement also is a well-known, widely distributed

Figure 13

Our Credo

We believe our first responsibility is to the doctors, nurses and patients,
to mothers and fathers and all others who use our products and services.
In meeting their needs everything we do must be of high quality.
We must constantly strive to reduce our costs
in order to maintain reasonable prices.
Customers' orders must be serviced promptly and accurately.
Our suppliers and distributors must have an opportunity
to make a fair profit.

We are responsible to our employees,
the men and women who work with us throughout the world.
Everyone must be considered as an individual.
We must respect their dignity and recognize their merit.
They must have a sense of security in their jobs.
Compensation must be fair and adequate,
and working conditions clean, orderly and safe.
We must be mindful of ways to help our employees fulfill
their family responsibilities.
Employees must feel free to make suggestions and complaints.
There must be equal opportunity for employment, development
and advancement for those qualified.
We must provide competent management,
and their actions must be just and ethical.

We are responsible to the communities in which we live and work
and to the world community as well.
We must be good citizens — support good works and charities
and bear our fair share of taxes.
We must encourage civic improvements and better health and education.
We must maintain in good order
the property we are privileged to use,
protecting the environment and natural resources.

Our final responsibility is to our stockholders.
Business must make a sound profit.
We must experiment with new ideas.
Research must be carried on, innovative programs developed
and mistakes paid for.
New equipment must be purchased, new facilities provided
and new products launched.
Reserves must be created to provide for adverse times.
When we operate according to these principles,
the stockholders should realize a fair return.

Johnson & Johnson

document, though of relatively recent origin (1985). Here is the text of "Our Commitments:"

- To our customers we will be attentive and strive to maximize the value, quality and operability of the company's products and services.
- To our suppliers we will be the best customer we can be and will emphasize both fair competition and long-lasting relationships.
- To the many communities of which we are a member, and to society as a whole, we will act as responsible and responsive corporate citizens and in a moral, ethical and beneficial manner.
- To our shareholders we will pursue our growth and earnings objectives while always keeping ethical standards at the forefront of our activities.
- And, as employees, we will treat one another fairly and with the dignity and respect due all human beings.

Another Commitment Statement

This statement is issued as part of a booklet on Standards of Business Conduct. First comes a brief summary of the company's commitments, "which form a basis for its standards."

The standards themselves are not organized either by commitments or by responsibilities. They are followed by a proportionately sizable part on interpretation and implementation of the standards, mostly in a question-and-answer format. "If you believe that an action you are about to take may be in conflict with the Standards of Business Conduct, or falls somewhere in the gray area between right or wrong, consult your supervisor before taking such action. *If in doubt — please ask.*" A condensed version of the commitments follows:

SHAREHOLDERS: We will maintain high ethical standards while pursuing sales and earnings growth. We will treat our shareholders fairly in all respects and will consider their interests in our actions.

EMPLOYEES: We will provide our employees with equitable compensation, good working conditions and an environment for growth. Our goal is to provide continuity of employment for productive, dedicated and loyal employees.

CUSTOMERS: We will provide customers with competitive quality products and services on a consistent and continuing basis. Relationships with our customers are to be ethical, responsible and in compliance with applicable laws.

COMMUNITY: We will be a responsible participant in the local, national and international communities in which we operate. We will stress good citizenship and corporate leadership.

SUPPLIERS: We will develop and maintain mutually beneficial relationships with suppliers. Relationships with our suppliers are to comply with all laws, regulations and ethical standards.

Concluding Observations

The two companies referred to above are in the same business, but one (the latter) is smaller. It is not, however, in the small-company category (the market value of its common shares is well over $1 billion).

The two commitment statements refer to the same five corporate constituencies: customers, employees, shareholders, communities, and suppliers, though not in the same order. One might interpret the difference as an indication of the degree of ethical concerns regarding the respective constituencies or as an ordering in terms of their importance to the companies.

The statement of the smaller company is longer and perhaps more carefully prepared. This company's board of directors has established an ethics committee of the board to oversee the company's administration of its standards. Of the five committee members, only one, the CEO, is not an outside director. In addition, the CEO chairs a management committee established by the board to assure compliance and to resolve concerns. A director of business conduct has been appointed, and each operating unit has a business standards liaison officer.

The larger company's booklet does not incorporate a question-and-answer section. There is an ethics program director at each company location. The company also has designated "a number" of staff personnel to assist the employees in resolving any questions involving ethics and conduct. Of course, the company's attorneys are also available, for assistance, information, and interpretative opinions.

Any or all of those ethics-associated organizational differences may have had a bearing on the commitment statement differences. Some of the differences also may be related to the consulting "ethicists," if any, who were contacted or contracted by the two companies.

The field of ethics, as a major corporate concern, encompasses a variety of approaches. It is still largely in an experimental stage, though many companies have had many years of experience.

Perhaps another factor accounting for some of the differences is the influence of the respective corporate cultures. One of the basic distinctions, in principle, between standards of conduct and corporate cultures is the notion of uniqueness or specificity or superiority, which is essential to a corporate culture.

The distinction between standards and cultures facilitates our understanding of the reasons for the diversity in general. The differences

among the standards probably will remain forever, ju₎
other distinguishing features of corporate life have persist₋₋
years, such as organizational structures and managerial styles. They
also often reflect regional, industry, or ownership factors and influences,
as well as company size.

Corporate self-image and a rather informal sense of belonging to
something special can contribute substantially to the readiness to
accept and implement standards of conduct. In this context, corporate standards also have to be somewhat different from those in
any other company.

This quality of mutual reinforcement has been captured and used
well by some companies. They introduce standards of ethics as an
extension of their cultures or as a formalization of something that
already has been practiced for years.

Statements on Standards of Ethics

Subject and Design

Policy statements refer to the subject of ethics as policies on ethics,
codes of ethics, standards of ethics, standards of business conduct,
ethical standards, or corporate codes of conduct. Those issued as
booklets are entitled: Code of Ethics, Code of Business Conduct,
Standards of Business Conduct, Policies on Business Conduct, Business Conduct Guidelines. For the purposes of this report, we often
use "Standards of Ethics" and "Code of Ethics." These terms reflect
adequately the usual content of the corporate policy statements dealing
with ethics: the individual provisions (standards) and the complete
sets of standards (codes).

Most of the standards of business ethics stress the corporate
commitment to maintain integrity and high ethical standards. They
focus on certain areas of corporate practices where a corresponding
commitment by corporate employees is of particular importance.

The basic message aims at a corporate ethical climate consistent
with the professed corporate self-image and its commitments regarding
business practices, dealings, and relationships. Specifically covered
are the most sensitive areas: the ones that require extra diligence,
that offer opportunities for undesirable behavior, or that involve ethical
dilemmas or situations in which any below-standard actions or attitudes may be especially harmful.

Content and Format

About 40% of the sample companies with separately written policies on ethics have issued them in handy booklets intended for distribution to all employees. Almost all of those codes of ethics contain rules on conflicts of interest and related procedures. Many include compliance attachments such as affidavits or certificates of declaration and disclosure.

Statements on standards of ethics are now the chief way of communicating corporate policies on ethics, at least in large corporations. For this reason, corporate codes of ethics will be covered more fully in the next chapter.

Conflicts of Interest

The conflict-of-interest policy often is considered a part of the overall ethics policies. Conflict-of-interest concerns sometimes constitute the main part of ethics standards.

All major companies share the view that conflicts between an employee's activities or personal interests and the company interests are one of the most significant causes of concern with regard to proper business conduct. The guiding principle is that the employee's acts must be motivated by the best interests of the company. Anything that might be inconsistent with this principle constitutes an actual or potential conflict of interest or the appearance of a conflict of interest.

Companies uniformly prohibit conflicts of interest, unless an employee has obtained written company approval. Such a basic clause may appear within a code of ethics or in a separately issued policy. In either case, typical conflict-of-interest situations are described in considerable detail.

Chapter 6

Corporate Codes of Ethics

Standards of Ethics: An Overview

The standards of ethics of the companies in the research sample often are overwhelmed by procedural details. They give an impression of comprehensive treatments of the respective topics, but they are not meant to offer complete coverage. The same applies to descriptions of the various laws.

Introductory broad statements are full of general tenets and principles that appeal to the very best characteristics of the employees. Designed to be uplifting and motivational, they are in many cases consistent with the general content and tone of the specific standards. On the other hand, some broad statements are in sharp contrast with the company approach apparent in individual standards; the body of the code emphasizes the "no" rules and, in general, how to protect the company from employee misbehavior.

The overly prohibitive emphasis sometimes is stressed further by lengthy references to the applicable laws and related penalties. Many of those descriptions merely elaborate on things that should be clear as a matter of regular lawful behavior. Certain aspects of lawful behavior may involve ethical dilemmas, which are not identified in those blanket treatments of the regulatory side of business activities. Clearly, some codes were adopted originally in response to certain new, tougher laws.

The standards targeted against fraud rather than toward higher ethics in business dealings reflect the antifraud campaigns to a considerable degree. The connection is evident particularly in the standards adopted in the late '70s and in the recent adoptions or amendments by defense contractors.

One company's code of ethics is organized in two parts. The first part sets out basic principles that relate to the matters of vital importance. The second part, which is a set of guidelines, summarizes the company's observance of all the applicable laws and regulations. To the extent that the standards address employee interest, protection, or rights, they do so mostly as a matter of observance of the corresponding laws, though this observance may be couched in the company commitment terms. Fewer codes include standards covering conditions involving unwarranted on-the-job exposure to ethical risks, except for those primarily addressing the security measures taken to safeguard company property.

Application

Corporate codes apply to all employees, often explicitly including members of their boards of directors. Some companies also apply their codes to agents, temporary employees and consultants. Additional standards of ethics for specific areas of the organization appear in the respective policies rather than in the codes of ethics. Such additional standards are set out in more detail; they do not modify the company-wide standards.

Financial recording and reporting are not always addressed directly. This area is covered extensively within the policies on internal auditing and accounting controls. If mentioned at all, integrity of financial reporting usually is treated as a set of procedures to be followed. This is necessary, of course, but it does not convey to the employees an understanding of their roles. Some companies include provisions that transactions must be recorded as necessary to assure the resulting financial statements will conform to generally accepted accounting principles, while many companies simply include the basic legal requirements.

Much topical variety among codes of ethics exists, not only on the basis of the specific nature of individual business, but also among companies engaged in the same line of business. A few companies in heavily regulated fields of activity regard such regulations as standards of conduct.

Service Companies

Service companies, on the average, have more comprehensive codes of ethics than industrial companies. The codes of service companies often are expanded to include the risks associated with their special areas of concern. Banks, for instance, cover extensively: protection of the customers' privacy, separation of trust function activities from loan and investment decisions, fiduciary relationships, "tie-in arrangements," personal investments, and other personal and financial affairs of the employees (officers), including their marital obligations and personal appearance. The bank officers are expected to act in a manner appropriate to their positions and not to participate in any activity that would reflect poorly on the corporation.

Utilities (communications) stress privacy of communications, customer proprietary information, and computer systems and software packages; health; and safety. Airlines focus on procurement policy, compliance with antitrust laws, and conduct on the job.

Certain similarities notwithstanding, codes of ethics differ substantially among service companies within the same type of business. The differences are even more pronounced, especially in the basic approaches, than among the industrial companies.

Topics Not Covered

Some issues could be added and discussed as possible or even desirable topics for existing or new standards. Our assignment here, however, is not to describe what is not there. We will make some references to this question elsewhere in this report. Our specific purpose in this section is to give an overview of the information that was acquired.

Some corporate activities do not cause any major ethical dilemmas. Other areas involve ethical concerns or create minor ethical dilemmas only under certain infrequent circumstances. Such topics can be treated conveniently and adequately within a single general standard, as they sometimes are, but only in a few codes.

Many codes are put together in such a manner that it takes special effort to distinguish the standards from the text that precedes and follows them. As we study that text, we are not always sure whether we are interpreting correctly the intent of the companies. In some companies, a requirement to adhere to the highest ethical standards has the status of a standard or policy, while in other companies, such a broad statement is used to introduce the standards. Some aspects of this problem will be treated in the next section.

Ethics Programs

Structural Complexity

Codes of some companies are overburdened with material on the related organizational measures and training devices. There is an

elaborate maze of organizational and ornamental trappings, appoint-
ments, duties, authorities, and responsibilities and the relationships
and coordination among them. It all adds up to a very intricate
mechanism, something like a sophisticated house alarm system. At
some point, you are so well protected that you are not sure any longer
whether you know how to open your window without triggering some
device in the system.

In one company, for example, a complex apparatus has been set up
to function as the Ethics Program Organization: a committee appointed
by the board of directors, an ethics committee (called, in this instance,
the committee on corporate responsibility), and the corporate ethics
steering group, which reports periodically to the CEO. Under committee directions, industrial relations departments establish education and training procedures "to facilitate employee awareness and
understanding of the Ethics Program." All of this is complemented
by the creation of special positions to provide counsel and to work
with general managers.

The pertinent point here: The details of the organizational arrangements have no place in the booklet (brochure) on ethics, except for
the provisions telling the employee where to seek guidance in case of
need. The extensive coverage of those other matters, most of which
also are subject to frequent changes, relegates the standards themselves
to the status of an insert between the introductory admonishments
and the concluding educational promises and arrangements.

Given such a formidable organization, probably the individual employee does not feel any urgent need to read and try to understand
the standards or to ask others if he doesn't. It will all be done for him
and for her in the forthcoming days, weeks, or months. For the real
work has yet to begin in many a company.

In the course of a long training program, employees will be educated:
they will get the questions and answers; discussion meetings will be
held; programs will be delivered by lecturers (consultants) and/or
appear on the screens; there will be tapes and guidebooks. The employees may even learn how to forget their real problems and questions,
until the ethics programs are over. Yes, there is a reason for some
skepticism about such quasi-rehabilitative promotion of ethical
know-how.

Constructive Potential

Regardless of the occasional excessive zeal, it is likely that most of
the well-intended ethics programs will yield the expected results, not

only by helping the employees comprehend the standards and learn how to make use of the associated services provided by the company but also by contributing to better business conduct at a higher level of ethical awareness and consensus. It is our belief that such developments inevitably will influence employee performance and, among other things, raise the earnings per share.

Investment in ethics is a good business proposition. As more and more companies develop similar programs, the similarity of ethical conditions also will facilitate personnel mobility, be it in the normal course of business or through acquisitions.

Right now, ethics programs are gaining more attention and recognition in our society. We have no doubt that the corporate ethics programs are here to stay. From time to time, also, ways will be found to regenerate the initial enthusiasm and momentum.

Compliance and Implementation

Compliance

Codes of ethics commonly include provisions for their administration and application. They also provide guidance regarding employee responsibilities, violations, and disciplinary consequences.

Each employee is required to seek counsel and interpretation or approval in case of doubt and also to report on any noncompliance. Failure to report may in itself be considered a violation. Standards also often indicate that certain types of actions are to be avoided, although they are not covered specifically.

Some companies have instituted additional organizational means and procedures, such as a corporate ethics committee, a "hotline" phone, a compliance review board, or an "ombudsman." Under ordinary circumstances, however, an employee refers to the immediate superior, internal auditing, or legal departments for guidance in matters of ethics.

Few companies include descriptions of the basic disciplinary procedures. There are rarely any direct references to the protective measures for those who report noncompliance, to the shared responsibility of the supervisor who condoned or even approved the alleged violations, or to the initial misinterpretation by the legal counsel.

Some codes of ethics have separate sections on administration or implementation or compliance or updating. An illustration is shown as Figure 14. It is a composite, compiled from several codes of ethics.

Figure 14

Code of Ethics: Application Procedures

Administration: Overall administration of this Code of Ethics is the responsibility of the CEO of the company. All amendments have to be recommended by the Audit Committee and approved by the Board of Directors. The CEO or his designate will be responsible for the dissemination, administration, and enforcement of this Code, will issue interpretations, guidelines, or relevant materials as appropriate, and will report to the Audit Committee all significant events related to the policies in the Code.

Whenever prior approval must be obtained or disclosure must be made under this Code and the CEO (or a relative of the CEO) has a personal involvement or interest in the situation, the CEO shall obtain prior approval from the Board of Directors.

Implementation: All officers, division directors, and departmental managers are responsible for the enforcement within their specific areas of supervisory responsibility. Such responsibilities include the periodic distribution of reports to, and the review thereof with, employees under their supervision.

Compliance: Regular audits of the company will include procedures to test compliance with the Code. The Board of Directors, Audit Committee, or executive management can order special audits of compliance. Appropriate officers and employees will be required periodically to certify their compliance with the requirements of this Code.

Updating: Periodical reviews and appropriate changes will be made. Employees will be fully informed.

Every employee has a personal responsibility ("an affirmative obligation") to uphold all standards in the code of ethics. Many companies also specify, within their codes or separately, one or more attendant responsibilities, such as: to be alert to any situation that appears to involve a conflict or impropriety, to resolve any doubt before taking an action, and to cooperate with auditors, both internal and external.

In many companies, employees are required to file a signed statement, annually or from time to time, as to their understanding of and compliance with the code. Companies often use detailed forms for special statements, such as declarations and disclosures of conflicts of interest, called certificates, affidavits, questionnaires, or verifications. Sometimes the procedure is simplified and a brief response form is used to establish whether a report is required or a statement has to be filed—only by managers or by all "key people."

Violations or suspected violations of codes of ethics usually are investigated. Suitable actions are taken as appropriate. Most codes of the participating companies refer to the reporting of violations and to the actions that may be taken. Most codes also require that employees report all violations. Some companies state that failure to do so can in itself be considered a violation.

Some companies refer separately to various sections of the code and respective actions. One company's code shows a listing of fraudulent acts divided into dishonest acts and criminal acts.

Implementation

Implementation entails a number of coordinated policies, procedures, and actions related to: dissemination (distribution), monitoring and reporting, interpretation, enforcement, periodical reviewing, and updating. Very few corporate codes cover all aspects of implementation. Some codes contain no references to implementation other than the requirement that employees comply with the code.

Most codes of ethics are distributed to all employees. It is primarily their managers' responsibility to make sure that they understand the code. As a rule, all managers are responsible for taking reasonable actions to assure that employees reporting to them adhere to the code.

Some old-fashioned companies make it plain that they issue a brochure on corporate standards not only for the employees but also for the other constituencies. Here is an example from a company's "Employee Code of Business Conduct":

> This booklet has been created to provide each employee with a set of guidelines:
> 1. So that present and prospective employees acting for the company will know how we wish to conduct our business.
> 2. So that people and organizations which have business dealings with the company will be aware of those principles which guide the company's employees in their day-to-day business operations.

Sound business reasoning leads to the conviction that the company's interests may be served well by a wide circulation of its standards of conduct. Such an approach gives the company an "ethics edge," especially if the company's practices are generally consistent with its professed self-image. This type of reasoning also would rule out any unnecessary detail on the current schedules and programs, unless they are permanent in nature and the details are not so excessive that they would interfere with the basic content and purpose.

Policies on Conflicts of Interest

It would not be feasible for a company to formulate in advance an all-inclusive set of possible conflict-of-interest situations and circumstances. The conflict-of-interest policies or standards therefore provide guidelines regarding such situations. In case of doubt, such occurrences have to be disclosed.

Disclosure and approval procedures vary among companies in the research sample. Usually, a questionnaire must be filed, whether or not any situation or activity requires approval. In many companies, questionnaires on conflicts of interest are distributed to all employees, especially when this topic is included in the code of ethics.

Principal Conflict Areas

Figure 15 shows a concise set of standards on conflict of interest, taken from Company A's corporate code of conduct. The annual certification also is attractively simple. Each executive, manager, or supervisor (more than 2,000 persons) receives a letter from the chairman of the board, who is the CEO as well, with the attached statement to be signed and returned to him.

The main areas covered in Figure 15 are included in the conflict-of-interest standards or policies of almost all other companies in the research sample. Many companies cover some additional areas and/or describe the conflict concerns more extensively, as will be illustrated in the other figures.

The conflict-of-interest standards in Figure 16, from Company B's code of ethics, are substantially condensed. In their original form, these standards are much more detailed than those of Company A, especially with respect to employees' relatives. This topic also is treated rather extensively in many other conflict-of-interest standards.

The topic of insider knowledge or information is covered elsewhere in the codes of both companies, as a separate standard. Company B requires no separate conflict-of-interest certification, only for the code in its entirety.

Figure 17 differs in format and style from Figures 15 and 16. This is a policy on conflict of interest (abbreviated) from a company's code of business conduct.

Figure 18 has been structured by the researcher to include a declaration of no conflict-of-interest involvement and a disclosure statement of possible conflicts of interest.

Taken together, the examples contain or refer to a wide range of areas. No single company covers all of them, and certainly it would be difficult to find companies giving a similar degree of emphasis to each of the commonly covered conflict-of-interest areas.

This variety contains a quality element. It is apparent that every company views its own needs in accordance with the notion of the prevailing corporate ethical climate rather than taking the easier approach of adopting some widespread pattern of form or substance.

Figure 15

Conflict-of-Interest Standards: Company A

1. Employees are forbidden to have direct or indirect ownership interests (excluding publicly traded securities of large companies listed on a stock exchange) or profit participation in organizations selling or buying goods or services to or from the Company where such relationship may reasonably lead to a conflict of interest.
2. Employees or members of their families may not receive compensation, services, gifts, or entertainment from such organizations which receipt could reasonably be construed to have influenced the employee in dealing with them on behalf of the Company.
3. In accordance with Personnel Policy, "Outside Employment", the Company prohibits its employees from engaging in outside employment with a supplier, customer, competitor, or a firm that may become such in the foreseeable future where such relationship may reasonably lead to a conflict of interest.
4. Certain employees will be required to sign a "Conflict of Interest Statement" letter annually.
5. Employees who have questions regarding what constitutes a conflict of interest should discuss the matter with their division management.

Figure 16

Conflict-of-Interest Standards: Company B

1. No employee or Director should engage in any activity or have any relationship which could conflict with or be contrary to the best interests of the Company. It is expected that each employee's entire working abilities will be available to the Company.
2. No employee may use his or her Company position or title in connection with outside activities, nor may any employee do anything which might infer sponsorship or support by the Company of such activities (with the exception of social service and community activities), or use any Company equipment,

Figure 16 (continued)

supplies or facilities in connection with outside activities, unless such use has been approved by the employee's immediate supervisor.

3. Investment in, ownership of, or any other personal association (either by the employee or members of his immediate family) with an actual or potential supplier, customer, or competitor, may create a conflict of interest. If any such circumstance results in the employee possibly having influence over the business dealings of such supplier, customer or competitor, or if the employee's position with the Company is such that he or she could influence a decision in any way with respect to Company dealings with such supplier, customer or competitor, permission for the initiation or continuation of such circumstance must be obtained from the employee's immediate supervisor.

4. An employee must not, directly or indirectly, acquire or hold real property, leaseholds, patents, or other property or rights in which the Company has, or the employee knows or has reason to believe at the time of acquisition that the Company is likely to have, an interest.

5. Sons, daughters, spouses, and close relatives of an employee may apply for full-time employment. Such applications will be evaluated on the same basis as all other applicants. If hired, such persons should not, except in very special circumstances, report to a parent or close relative, and, preferably, should be in a section of the Company outside of a parent's or relative's area of supervision.

6. An employee must neither solicit nor accept from suppliers, customers, or others dealing with the Company, gifts, loans, fees, services or entertainment which is of sufficient value that its acceptance might be construed as influencing the conduct of business.

Figure 17
Conflict-of-Interest Policy

Employees of the Company should have no relationship, financial or otherwise, with any supplier or competitor that might be construed as a conflict of interest, or that might even appear to impair their independence of judgment on behalf of their company.

Gifts, loans, unusual hospitality, or any other thing of monetary value that could influence actions, or give the appearance of being capable of influencing actions should not be accepted. Unsolicited gifts should be promptly reported to your supervisor and then returned to the donor, if possible, or disposed of in another appropriate manner.

Since each employee has a primary obligation to his or her employer, any form of outside activity, including employment or self-employment, must be kept totally separate from, and not interfere with, his or her company employment. No outside activity should involve the use of company assets, funds,

Figure 17 (continued)

materials, facilities, or the services of other company employees unless properly authorized.

Employees should avoid any outside activity that could adversely affect the independence and objectivity of their judgment, interfere with the timely and effective performance of their duties and responsibilities, or that could conflict, or appear to conflict, with the best interests of our Company. Of course, employees should not use their positions with the Company for outside gain or benefit, nor should they use proprietary or other confidential or private company information in any outside activity.

An actual—or even a potential—conflict of interest should be discussed promptly with your supervisor or your Legal Department.

Figure 18
Declaration and Disclosure of Conflict of Interest
June 25, 1989

DECLARATION
I have read and I understand the Company's Policy on Conflicts of Interest (Policy):

1. _____ In the past 12 months, I have had no reason to submit a Disclosure Statement. If a potential conflict of interest should arise in the future, I will immediately eliminate it or promptly submit a Disclosure Statement.
2. _____ I am submitting a Disclosure Statement.

_____   _____   _____
Name (please PRINT)   Date   Signature

DISCLOSURE STATEMENT
1. Ownership or any financial participation: Yes_____ No_____
2. Compensation, gift, loan or other benefit received: Yes_____ No_____
3. Activity requiring the use of Company resources: Yes_____ No_____
4. Activity involving substantial time and/or effort: Yes_____ No_____
5. Position, relationship or anything else that might be or appear to be subject to disclosure and/or approval: Yes_____ No_____

I attach descriptions of each "Yes" item. I am applying for a ruling of its status with respect to the Policy and, if needed, an approval. It is my understanding that if a "Yes" item is not subject to disclosure and I am so notified by the Company, I will be entitled to consider it a "No" item in any future Disclosure Statement, unless a material change occurs regarding the respective item or the Policy. Description(s):

_____   _____   _____
Name (please PRINT)   Date   Signature

Concluding Observations

It has been one of the premises of this project that some latent ethics energy exists in every corporation, with the possible exception of the companies with the most complacent, entrenched, or arrogant top management teams. Such complacency may be unduly encouraged as the ethics programs grow in size and effectiveness.

An ethics program cannot have a long-lasting impact unless the tone set at the top furnishes an example, primarily through the exemplary actions of top management. We refer here to the ethical side of top management's critical decisions, rather than to their public postures.

An illustration of the foregoing is Chrysler Corporation's former practice of disconnecting odometers on the cars given for test drives to assembly plant managers. It is a case that not only involves a posture-action confrontation but also demonstrates how difficult it sometimes is to make a proper-improper distinction. The following quotation is from an article by Thomas G. Donlan, "Still a Lousy Idea," *Barron's*, March 6, 1989, pp. 24-25:

> In the summer of 1987,...Chrysler had been caught disconnecting odometers on factory-fresh cars so that managers could take them home at night. The company called it test driving as part of a quality assurance program, but...A grand jury indicted Chrysler for mail and wire fraud and conspiracy.
>
> 'America, we apologize,' said Lee Iacocca...'Testing cars is a good idea. Disconnecting odometers is a lousy idea....'
>
> 'They've put forth two faces,' says an angry, frustrated assistant U.S. attorney, James K. Steitz. 'There is the public relations face and the face in court.' ....'Chrysler is trying to put forth a public face that shows they made full restitution to all the victims, when in fact that's not true.'
>
> 'What crime?' Iacocca says in his new book, *Talking Straight*... He makes it clear that his apologetic approach to the odometer case was a matter of marketing, not ethics.

Differences Among Corporate Codes

Do the differences among the codes of ethics reflect some identifiable factors or circumstances? We commented earlier on the observed connection between codes and some developments that may have influenced the adoption of a code of ethics or its timing. Among other reasons, to the extent that they could be identified, are: (1) recent unfavorable experience within the company, (2) attempts to reverse the downtrend in company performance, and (3) pressure due to the recent widely publicized occurrences of unethical behavior in other companies, especially in the same industry or type of activity.

Companies with favorable ethics-related experience and good longer-term performance records tend to put their codes in a narrative style. They describe their views and ways of doing business, though with the focus on the expectations as to employee conduct. Almost casually, the employee is warned to watch out for possible pitfalls along the way, and the various laws and policies are called to his or her attention. The disciplinary actions for violations are the consequence of pursuing other than the regular company team player style.

In fact, such codes are formalized expositions of corporate cultures. They serve as effective communication or introduction devices, except that they are somewhat ambiguous as to the ways of rectifying or resolving the dilemmas caused by situational pressures.

Cause-and-Effect Relationships

A strong and pervasive sense of ethics is not indicative of the company's management style. A pattern of highly ethical conduct may be developed and maintained under the firm leadership of a CEO with an authoritarian or paternalistic attitude, in a company with a strong headquarters orientation or a highly decentralized one.

The topics covered reflect the company experience and its management's main concerns. Both may be related either to heavy exposure to internal fraud or to a high degree of exposure to external nonmarket forces and pressures and to the need of maintaining a favorable "good citizen" corporate reputation.

There is no indication that management teams are thinking of a higher level of ethics as a means of solidifying their defenses against "hostile" takeovers. Some of the measures taken by upper-level managements often appear focused on their own executive interests though they also may be beneficial to shareholders.

In this section and elsewhere, we have mentioned various factors or circumstances that cause or contribute to decisions regarding company codes of ethics. It seems reasonable to assume that these decisions have made certain things happen or prevented some events that otherwise would have occurred.

We could not find a suitable and reliable way of measuring the impact of a new code of ethics on company performance, other than some effects pertinent mostly to the immediate causes that triggered its adoption.

CPAs are adopting stricter rules and accepting extended responsibilities. Those efforts and actions do not necessarily call for material changes in their professional ethics, but anything positively influencing the effectiveness of controls has an important place in company considerations regarding ethics. Just as fraud detection may have a powerful impact on the subsequent occurrences of fraud, so does everything that narrows the range of opportunities for unethical actions of any kind.

Saying that the increased likelihood of detection has preventive or deterrent effects is nothing new. What is relatively new is the recognition of the equally evident effects of a high-level corporate ethical climate. Such a climate is even superior to direct controls as a preventive condition, because an ethically favorable set of circumstances acts as a support and reinforcement for those who normally conduct themselves properly but who still occasionally remain exposed to ethical dilemmas and associated risks.

Chapter 7

Corporate Records and Reports

Recording and Processing

Much of the attention paid to a company management's responsibility is centered on the final stage — the preparation and disclosure of financial statements. It is at this stage that a single management decision can have a material effect in terms of integrity of the company's financial reporting. Some of the ethical questions pertain mostly to the dilemmas arising at that level where the key decisions are made. These decisions involve the upper-level executives directly and reflect their levels of ethical conduct.

In this context, the underlying recording and processing structure of corporate accounting often is not considered a major area of ethical significance. Companies are required by law to maintain adequate records and to have the basic information processed in accordance with regulations and company-prescribed policies and procedures. Almost no company is without some system of internal auditing, with responsibilities ranging from establishing controls over the recording and processing system to the ongoing examination of its proper functioning.

The main intent here is to call the attention of managers directly in charge of these corporate functions — management accountants — to the ethical side of their work. We also want to point out that their responsibilities are of essential importance in terms of integrity of financial reporting at the corporate level. While many individual decisions may not seem to have any far-reaching effects, the cumulative impact is often equal to or greater than the impact of the final report preparation decisions. Subjective judgments are involved not only at the overall interpretation and presentation stage but also in the processes of recording and processing.

Responsibility of Management Accountants

Professional competence and subjective judgment are required to establish and maintain a recording system that will record all necessary items in adequate financial terms. Considerable analytical work is needed in many instances. Consistency is a key element.

Another important purpose of management accounting is to organize the recording and processing in such a way that the data can be put together readily as the information for decision-making purposes. It is not unusual to find that some of the conflicting views in the course of decision making are based on differing interpretations and uses of management accounting data.

Reporting

For Management Decision Making

Management accountants may tailor their reports to suit a particular manager's needs and preferences. A manager probably could get the data directly from the database through his or her computer, but a report prepared by management accounting personnel tends to have the content and the appearance of an unbiased and, more credible document.

The life of management accountants of course has additional bility — to the corporate office and to the management of the particular division, subsidiary, or plant. Management accounting reporting has to be designed to facilitate the work of all operating managers. Attempts to match the reports to an individual manager's behavior easily can create some discrepancies and ethical dilemmas.

The management accounting code of ethics (see Figure 19) is certainly helpful as to the recognition of various situations involving professional ethical dilemmas, as well as being a set of guidelines. The code of ethics also may provide considerable encouragement and support, especially in dealings with those who respect the professional standards of ethics. On the other side, the existence of a code of ethics for management accounting does not necessarily inhibit a demanding executive who prefers a different interpretation of standards of professional conduct or who simply chooses to ignore them. The code cannot give management accountants an additional capacity to correct such situations or to resolve consequent ethical dilemmas in conformity with the ethics in the code. Under some circumstances, which probably are rare, the existence of a professional code may only add still another tier of responsibility.

Figure 19
Standards of Ethical Conduct for Management Accountants

Management accountants have an obligation to the organizations they serve, their profession, the public, and themselves to maintain the highest standards of ethical conduct. In recognition of this obligation, the National Association of Accountants has promulgated the following standards of ethical conduct for management accountants. Adherence to these standards is integral to achieving the *Objectives of Management Accounting.*[1] Management accountants shall not commit acts contrary to these standards nor shall they condone the commission of such acts by others within their organizations.

Competence

Management accountants have a responsibility to:
- Maintain an appropriate level of professional competence by ongoing development of their knowledge and skills.
- Perform their professional duties in accordance with relevant laws, regulations, and technical standards.
- Prepare complete and clear reports and recommendations after appropriate analyses of relevant and reliable information.

Confidentiality

Management accountants have a responsibility to:
- Refrain from disclosing confidential information acquired in the course of their work except when authorized, unless legally obligated to do so.
- Inform subordinates as appropriate regarding the confidentiality of information acquired in the course of their work and monitor their activities to assure the maintenance of that confidentiality.
- Refrain from using or appearing to use confidential information acquired in the course of their work for unethical or illegal advantage either personally or through third parties.

Integrity

Management accountants have a responsibility to:
- Avoid actual or apparent conflicts of interest and advise all appropriate parties of any potential conflict.

---

[1]National Association of Accountants, *Statements on Management Accounting: Objectives of Management Accounting,* Statement No. 1B, June 17, 1982.

Figure 19 (continued)

- Refrain from engaging in any activity that would prejudice their ability to carry out their duties ethically.
- Refuse any gift, favor, or hospitality that would influence or would appear to influence their actions.
- Refrain from either actively or passively subverting the attainment of the organization's legitimate and ethical objectives.
- Recognize and communicate professional limitations or other constraints that would preclude responsible judgment or successful performance of an activity.
- Communicate unfavorable as well as favorable information and professional judgments or opinions.
- Refrain from engaging in or supporting any activity that would discredit the profession.

Objectivity

Management accountants have a responsibility to:
- Communicate information fairly and objectively.
- Disclose fully all relevant information that could reasonably be expected to influence an intended user's understanding of the reports, comments, and recommendations presented.

Resolution of Ethical Conflict

In applying the standards of ethical conduct, management accountants may encounter problems in identifying unethical behavior or in resolving an ethical conflict. When faced with significant ethical issues, management accountants should follow the established policies of the organization bearing on the resolution of such conflict. If these policies do not resolve the ethical conflict, management accountants should consider the following course of action:
- Discuss such problems with the immediate superior except when it appears that the superior is involved, in which case the problem should be presented initially to the next higher managerial level. If satisfactory resolution cannot be achieved when the problem is initially presented, submit the issues to the next higher managerial level. If the immediate superior is the chief executive officer, or equivalent, the acceptable reviewing authority may be a group such as the audit committee, executive committee, board of directors, board of trustees, or owners. Contact with levels above the immediate superior should be initiated only with the superior's knowledge, assuming the superior is not involved.
- Clarify relevant concepts by confidential discussion with an objective advisor to obtain an understanding of possible courses of action.
- If the ethical conflict still exists after exhausting all levels of internal review, the management accountant may have no other recourse on significant matters than to resign from the organization and to submit an

Figure 19 (continued)

informative memorandum to an appropriate representative of the organization.
Except where legally prescribed, communication of such problems to authorities or individuals not employed or engaged by the organization is not considered appropriate.

Financial Statements

Corporate financial statements are prepared from the same records and by the same processes as the reports intended primarily for management decision making. They may, however, pose additional ethical dilemmas not necessarily present in the reporting for management decision purposes.

Corporate financial statements disclose a corporation's financial dimensions in conformity with the applicable requirements. These requirements are mutually compatible, although they may reflect views that differ somewhat as to the relative emphasis or the degree of concern regarding one or another of the multipurpose functions of financial statements.

Integrity is a universally accepted criterion. It means primarily that the financial statements are complete and not misleading in any material respect. Yet the principle of completeness is subject to some subjective judgments, and its practical side has been one of the issues faced occasionally by the Accounting Standards Board. The status of the impact-of-inflation disclosures is but one example of the never-ending effect of changing circumstances on the rules that, cumulatively, represent the interpretation of the principle of completeness.

In practice, the principle of completeness raises the question of an appropriate choice among all the possible components and extensions, each of which could be considered useful to some segment of the investing public. The doctrine of users' primacy, which is prevalent, does not by itself offer a reliable basis or guide regarding the differences in the users' needs or the degree of preference be accorded to any particular homogeneous group of users or potential users.

The presently dominant view is that the financial statements are used primarily by the reasonably "sophisticated" segments of the investing public. A natural consequence, then, is to give those select users a certain preference in terms of both the content and the level of presentation.

It does appear that the complexity of financial statements already exceeds the comprehension level of the "average" shareholder. If this is correct, then the further consequences of the dominant view become irrelevant, except for some ethical connotations and, perhaps, the old-fashioned accounting doctrine of fairness. The standards-setting body even may design a condensed version for the "small" investor.

So far in this section, the "not misleading" attribute of integrity has not been covered. In a work on ethics, it requires a more extensive coverage than the topic of completeness and so will be treated in a separate section.

To conclude, the notion of completeness refers to the output of the financial recording, processing, and reporting structure. Other information, which also may be of vital significance, does not appear in the financial statements. Some of it may be found elsewhere in the annual meeting materials, such as proxy statements.

Fraud in Financial Reporting

The term "fraud" has an amorphous meaning. It covers a wide spectrum of dishonest or deceitful behavior in a variety of situations. A fraud does not necessarily constitute a crime.

The elements of fraudulent behavior generally include the use of deception as a means of gaining a dishonest advantage over someone else. Fraud encompasses many types of deception and gains — from unfair competition to the fraudulent decisions made supposedly for the benefit of a company.

It is rare that an employee has no opportunity for fraudulent behavior, either by committing a fraud against the employer or against a third party. The presence of opportunity is a key factor, especially when combined with a low chance of detection or punishment if the fraud is detected.

Another key factor is motivation. Honesty is an individual trait that not only should be respected but also should be supported rigorously by company management. The most effective support comes from exemplary behavior on the part of the company's executives. It is also their duty to organize the employees' areas of responsibility in such a way that both the exposure to fraud and the temptation to commit fraud are reduced to an unavoidable minimum.

The Issue of "White-Collar" Fraud

So-called "white-collar" crime has been receiving increased attention, due to its potentially disastrous financial consequences. This area contains numerous opportunities not only for fraud but also for its concealment.

Many companies remain especially vulnerable with respect to computer fraud. Managements still tend to be oriented toward "traditional" forms of fraud and controls. Some managements simply do not understand the risks associated with high-technology information processing systems or tend to believe that auditors would detect any systematic fraud.

Fraudulent Records and Statements

Fraud that takes place anywhere in a company, individually or cumulatively, may have a material impact on its financial results. Unless detected and recorded, such fraud would render the company's financial statements fraudulent.

Protection of the company's property is a prime fiduciary responsibility of its management. Moreover, the perceived integrity of the financial statements makes it mandatory, as a matter of public trust, for company managements to establish and maintain adequate security and control systems.

Inadvertent or intentional acts that result in misrepresentation may occur at any stage or level preceding the preparation of a company's annual report. Those activities take place throughout a company, including its relationships or contacts with suppliers, customers, governmental officials and agencies (domestic and foreign), financial institutions, news media, and, of course, its competitors. Some of those activities are not, by themselves, financial in nature but they ultimately may have a fraudulent impact on the financial statements. Even those activities that are financial may involve matters not covered by the financial reporting structure and the related financial (accounting and auditing) control systems of the company.

Containment of Fraud

An organizational climate conducive to honesty in all relationships and dealings acts as a powerful, all-pervasive deterrent to fraud. Such a climate has a salutary impact even on those few who otherwise might be inclined to stretch their principles to accommodate a certain "acceptable" degree of dishonesty, such as using company facilities for personal purposes or wasting time during the workday. Company policies should be as specific as practicable in order to make a clear distinction between the acceptable or tolerable and the fraudulent, particularly in some areas of exposure or temptation such as gifts and entertainment.

Some "gray" areas of business conduct cannot be covered effectively by company policies, no matter how detailed. In those areas of enforcing the unenforceable, there is no substitute for a well-ingrained sense of business ethics.

Fraud committed in unrecorded transactions does not require manipulation of accounts. Fraud concealment that requires a falsification of reports or records often involves someone with direct access to them and/or the complicity of someone who has access. The perpetrators usually are skilled employees who are also familiar with the internal controls.

Fraud concealment happens chiefly when the situation creates a favorable climate for it. It can be contained through diligent control and company support of high standards of ethics.

Executive Fraud

There is no convincing evidence that corporate executives are any more or less prone to fraudulent behavior than other employees even though they have opportunities not open to lower-level employees. Executives could gain certain dishonest advantages through seemingly legitimate decisions.

On the other hand, many of the possible motivational factors for fraud are absent at the executive level, so it is not likely that executives would engage in fraud.

One major exception to this is fraud committed by means of executive decisions that are designed expressly to change the results reported in the company's financial statements. This type of fraud can be committed indirectly, through decisions whose effect causes fraudulent financial statements, or it can take place within the financial reporting structure directly. The latter kind of fraud cannot be carried out unless it is condoned or activated by accounting or auditing professionals.

The Practice of "Earnings Management"

A common purpose of misleading or incomplete financial reporting is to "manage" corporate earnings so as to maintain a favorable trend consistent with stock market expectations and with optimal levels of the executive incentive compensation. It is a widespread and well-known practice that has been exposed, documented, analyzed, and sharply criticized over the years in numerous write-ups, from the prominently headlined news items to the detailed analyses in articles and books.

A misrepresentation involving company executives is likely to have a significant impact on the reported earnings, often great enough to constitute a fraud, though not a crime. Under regular conditions, the misrepresentation "corrects" the level of reported earnings in the desired direction. The earnings are bolstered in a year of poor, substandard operating results. In an exceptionally good year, the earnings may be adjusted downward, sometimes to offset earlier corrective measures but more often to delay the reporting of income and thus make it available in the next year when it may be needed to offset an unfavorable change in operating results.

Short-Term Pressures: Internal

Short-term orientation is a well-established characteristic of management attitudes and practices in many, probably most, business enterprises. Many works on the subject have demonstrated that the short-term emphasis results in a less-than-optimal management performance over a longer term and in some cases may have detrimental consequences.

Some changes have been taking place in this respect. More top managements are becoming aware of the benefits of strategic planning and other tools designed to stress the longer-term aspects of executive decisions. This does not necessarily mean that the internal short-term pressures have been reduced.

Short-Term Pressures: External

The short-term orientation is partly attributable to external pressures. For a variety of reasons, the stockholders, big and small alike, and the stock market in general share the attitudes prevailing within companies. They prefer stability and a steady upward trend in reported earnings over a longer period of time, but they react, often out of proportion, to any "disappointments" in the short run.

By getting engaged in earnings management, corporate executives accommodate the expectations and interests of several company constituencies — shareholders and investors in general, financial analysts, investment advisors, and others, including creditors — and company employees to the extent that their compensation is affected by the market performance of company securities.

Their direct self-interest notwithstanding, corporate executives whose behavior was motivated or influenced by those other considerations may, indeed, relate the practice of earnings management to the best interests of their companies. In the absence of this practice, the price-earnings ratios for their company stocks would be lower than for similar companies with more reliable earnings patterns.

Accounting System

The practice of earnings management is facilitated by the conservative orientation (bias) of generally accepted accounting principles, as well as by the existence of some alternative treatments. The doctrine, or principle, of conservatism is conceptually a means of preserving the integrity of financial statements. On the other hand, its consistent asymmetry may cause a substantial understatement of corporate equity. This is not necessarily serving the best interests of corporate owners, current or potential.

A loss is readily recognized — its prompt recognition is even required in many situations — while a gain has to be realized first. Undervalued assets make it possible to show a higher rate of return on investment, that is, higher than it would be if assets were not undervalued. They also may be converted into cash to increase the reported earnings and/or to reduce the amount of corporate debt incurred in a leveraged buyout (LBO).

Diversification

In search of long-term solutions to the short-term market sensitivity, many companies have become diversified. There are many other reasons for diversification, of course, but by entering product or service markets with differing cyclical patterns, companies can maintain earnings stability to a substantial degree.

In principle, this is a sound approach. Ethically, it does not even belong in the section referring to earnings management practices, most of which involve some degree of questionable behavior.

As to the expected balancing or smoothing effects of diversification on the year-to-year earnings per share, the experience of many companies has been less than satisfactory. Moreover, acquisition and/or disinvestment tactics and strategies nowadays often serve a variety of purposes other than to prevent fluctuations of company earnings or for the sake of a steady cash flow.

Tax Considerations

Tax-related considerations frequently are present in decisions that appear to have been made for "noneconomic" purposes. To a corporation or any taxpayer, a favorable tax treatment is a valid factor in the decision-making process, regardless of whether a given preferential treatment is justifiable.

Causes and Effects

A transaction made or recorded and reported with intention to commit a fraudulent act impairs the integrity of financial reporting. Integrity also may be impaired when no such intention exists.

It is difficult to segregate decisions made for economic reasons from the decisions intended for other purposes. The short-term pressures and other factors have been used by many to explain or justify a variety of questionable practices.

The public takes fraudulent or questionable financial statements at face value because of their perceived integrity. Management's actual performance is one of the key facts, to be shown as clearly as possible. Anything designed to cause a false impression is less than satisfactory. In most cases, a careful examination of all materials contained in the annual reports, if done by an expert analyst, results in reliable figures or, if the company value remains unrecognized, the acquisition process may bring about the necessary correction.

Chapter 8

Corporate Disclosure System

Corporate Governance

A public company is owned and controlled by the holders of the voting shares issued by the company. The elected board of directors usually includes several "outside" members. They do not hold management positions within the company and are, therefore, presumably more independent in their judgments and voting patterns than the board members who also serve on the company's management team. This is the main reason for the widely observed emphasis on their participation in the company's control mechanisms.

The outside board members often are on the company's audit committee. In some companies, all persons serving on the audit and similar committees, such as ethics committees, are outside board members.

Disclosures to Shareholders and Others

The corporate disclosure system is of critical importance to shareholders, and management reporting to shareholders is a statutory responsibility fully observed by almost all public companies. Shareholders usually receive quarterly and audited annual reports. In addition, well-managed companies keep their shareholders informed of any interim management actions considered of immediate interest to them. This also is customary for any other material changes and developments, though such announcements may not be required.

The prevailing patterns of company communications to shareholders and others are valuable indicators of the ethical climate in a company. Both the frequency and content are significant. Some additional insight may be acquired simply by comparing those communications with the promotional market-targeted campaigns and general public relations releases.

Public companies have access to securities and capital markets. This entails management responsibility for adequate disclosure, which is not identical to the corporate governance disclosure system except in terms of integrity. The disclosures intended for specific purposes other than for reporting to shareholders are governed by the needs and requirements of the respective constituencies or by the nature of the matters subject to reporting obligations, regulatory and/or contractual.

Voting/Decision Power Structure

A corporation ultimately is run by its shareholders (or by holders of preferred shares, under certain conditions). In practice, however, corporate governance is sometimes more symbolic than real, especially with respect to certain short-term management decisions that may have or even are designed to have far-reaching consequences. Such structural defects of corporate governance cannot be remedied adequately by stricter auditing standards. Additional disclosure rules or more forceful implementation of the existing ones hardly can prevent an unethical management team from shortchanging its shareholders through a variety of actions that are not illegal and, perhaps, do not even appear questionable at the time to any uninitiated observers. A favorable corporate ethical climate appears to be the only means that offers some real hope.

A company's overall organizational setup is conditioned in many ways by the regulations/statutes of the state in which it is incorporated. In a relatively permissive state, a company is allowed considerable latitude in certain matters that may be of particular concern to management. Sometimes either the company preferences or the regulatory climate change over time, so companies occasionally "move" to a more congenial state.

Our concern here is with those incorporation-induced differences among companies that could have an impact on the company internal power structure, especially in terms of corporate governance. Those differences may leave the field open for possible attempts to commit unethical acts or to establish company practices that would have been ethically questionable in more restrictive states.

Differences among companies regarding the voting rights of shareholders also have ethical connotations in a growing number of cases. The power to control a company sometimes is retained for the holders of shares specifically designated as voting shares. The holders of other classes of shares have restricted voting rights or none at all.

The question of propriety regarding differing voting rights arises when a company's voting shares do not trade on the public markets or are held by only a few shareholders, whose total equity interest is disproportionately smaller than the equity contributed by the holders of nonvoting shares.

The "superstock" category of shares used to serve mainly as a device to preserve the controlling position of the company founding family. More recently, the same or similar privileges have been created in the attempts to acquire control regardless of shareholders' preferences. Some other tactics continually being developed in the ongoing struggle for corporate control — an outgrowth of the takeover phenomenon — also involve potential ethical dilemmas.

Entrenched corporate management also may use ethically questionable defensive tactics. Some changes affecting the voting rights of equity participants are not necessarily created as defensive means though they result in additional management power and, therefore, could be used as a defensive tool, if need be. The latest is the introduction of so-called unbundled stock units.

In extreme cases, managements appear to be giving only nominal recognition to their prime fiduciary duty to run the public company on behalf of its equity owners. As a result of a multitude of leveraged buyouts and the associated concerns, it is likely that some legislative and additional regulatory actions will be taken. The contemplated measures may not enhance the cause of corporate governance at all, though they may curb the power of company management. Perhaps someone will even try to revive or re-ignite the trusteeship concept — that corporate obligations to the public in general are to be given equal or preferential status in the context of company decision making.

Management Reporting to Shareholders

Annual Reports

In terms of legal and regulatory requirements, the financial sections are of critical importance. "Congress itself identified financial statements as an essential component of the disclosure system on which the U.S. securities markets are based." (From the report of the National Commission on Fraudulent Financial Reporting, p. 31 — see Appendix A-3.)

Many of the major corporations have developed annual reports into yet another corporate-culture ritual, producing impressive showpieces in terms of artistic design and other paraphernalia.

It is tempting to argue that this apparent contest among companies adds very little to the communication or reporting value of their annual reports, or that a form-over-substance effect may be the main result by detracting attention from the "cold" figures in the financial statements. On the other hand, it is plausible that the magazine format attracts the attention of the shareholders, who then might want to read the financial statements as well.

Management Responsibility Statements

A management report or statement of responsibility for financial statements now appears as a separate item in annual reports. It usually precedes the accountants' report. Some statements are presented with the signatures (CEO and CFO), while some are not signed.

Here are several examples of ethics-related passages:

1. The company's formally stated and communicated policies demand of employees high ethical standards in their conduct of business. These policies address, among other things, potential conflicts of interest; compliance with all domestic and foreign laws, including those related to financial disclosure; and the confidentiality of proprietary information.
2. The company's system of internal controls is...built on a business ethics policy which requires all employees to maintain the highest ethical standards in conducting company affairs.
3. The control process starts with the hiring and training of qualified people and then providing them with corporate objectives and policies that adhere to the highest principles of business ethics so that they understand how we expect them to conduct our business. Continuing education and training programs made available to all personnel serve to keep our basic goals and objectives in proper perspective.
4. As part of the internal control system, the company has a policy on Conflicts of Interest and a Code of Business Ethics. All directors, officers and key employees are required to submit annually a signed statement regarding compliance with these policies.
5. Management is responsible for conducting our business in an ethical,

moral manner assuring that our business practices encompass the highest, most uncompromising standards of personal and business conduct. These standards, which address conflict of interest, compliance with laws and acceptable business practices, and proper employee conduct, are included in our Code of Conduct. The importance of these standards is stressed throughout the company and all our employees are expected to comply with them.

Corporate Boards and Independent Auditors

The Role of Corporate Boards

Two different kinds of executive decisions relate to the practice of earnings management:

1. Actions designed to change the timing of decisions or transactions, decisions to convert asset appreciation into realized gains, or other decisions meant to cause changes in reported earnings.
2. Actions designed to establish a plausible rationale for a favorable accounting interpretation or to take advantage of the available choices among alternative tax or accounting treatments.

Integrity of financial reporting is one of the primary concerns of a company's board of directors. In recent years, audit committees have been formed to assume responsibility for this control function of the board. They often are made up solely of outside members of the board. (Some companies also have ethics committees.)

Judging from the evidence, audit committees are fairly active. They receive direct reports and/or maintain direct contact with both internal and external auditors.

It seems likely that audit committees are informed of the matters that refer to accounting rules and procedures. Conversely, it is less likely that upper executives would seek advice from audit committees regarding other actions that may affect financial reporting.

The Role of Auditors

The part auditors should have in detecting fraud or the degree of their responsibility regarding fraudulent financial reporting has been debated for many years. It was not until very recently (1988) that this responsibility has been accepted by the profession.

The expanded responsibility—to design their procedures actively toward a search for fraud—is reflected in a new standard letter from the independent public accountants, which appears in company annual reports:

> We have studied the accompanying balance sheets of X Company as of December 31, 19X2 and 19X1, and the related statements of income, retained earnings, and cash flows for the years then ended. These financial statements are the responsibility of the Company's management. Our responsibility is to express an opinion on those financial statements based on our audits. We conducted our audits in accordance with generally accepted auditing standards. Those standards require that we plan and perform the audit to obtain reasonable assurance about whether the financial statements are free of material misstatement. An audit includes examining, on a test basis, evidence supporting the amounts and disclosures in the financial statements. An audit also includes assessing the accounting principles used and significant estimates made by management, as well as evaluating the overall financial statement presentation. We believe that our audits provide a reasonable basis for our opinion. In our opinion, the financial statements referred to above present fairly, in all material respects, the financial position of X Company as of (at) December 31, 19X2 and 19X1, and the results of its operations and its cash flows for the years then ended in conformity with generally accepted accounting principles.
> (Signature)
> (Date)

Optional paragraph if the company is in financial trouble:

> The accompanying financial statements have been prepared assuming that Company Y will continue as a going concern. As discussed in Note X to the financial statements, Company Y has suffered recurring losses from operations and has a net capital deficiency that raise substantial doubt about the entity's ability to continue as a going concern. Management's plans in regard to these matters are also described in Note X. The financial statements do not include any adjustments that might result from the outcome of this uncertainty.

This change is a significant step among the recent developments and actions taken by the public accounting profession. It undoubtedly will help remove some differences within the profession, strengthen the external auditing process, and bring its impact closer to public expectations. The additions also will serve to explain the responsibilities of the profession. With fewer misconceptions, public expectations may be brought closer to a more realistic level.

Financial Reporting Abroad

Differences and Similarities

As with many other aspects of modern, increasingly interconnected and interdependent economic realities, the notion of uniformity has a great pragmatic appeal in questions concerning financial reporting standards and practices. Existing differences make it more difficult to run multinational companies and to develop coordinated economic efforts among the countries with compatible general political and/or economic structures. What is perhaps even more important, those differences are an undesirable obstacle to the intercountry flow of financial trade and investment capital resources.

Many people have been inclined to believe that a high degree of uniformity is an indisputable ultimate goal, but the currently prevailing view is that certain basic harmonization would be sufficient. Increased comparability of financial statements is one of the main immediate objectives.

The basic approaches to accounting and financial-reporting principles and practices in some countries are very similar. Much of this similarity can be traced to a common source in the past, as in the former colonial possessions of the United Kingdom and other European countries, or to the dominant influence of American standards in more recent years.

Harmonization Efforts

The significant progress toward harmonization is due partly to company recognition of the corresponding competitive advantages, either in dealings with the American companies, investment community, and regulatory bodies or in the corresponding activities in other countries. The International Accounting Standards Committee already has issued a series of statements to serve as guidelines. The European Common Market requirements, applicable to member countries, represent an important step in this direction. They will facilitate the planned economic integration. Such constructive developments also have been promoted by other international forums and agencies, including the United Nations.

A certain degree of uniformity has been achieved, indirectly as a side effect of some bilateral arrangements or directly as a result of compliance with the U.S. regulations and with the accounting standards. The regulations and standards are applicable to the foreign CPA practices, the U.S.-based multinational firms, and the foreign companies with substantial activities within the United States, such as those seeking listings on our stock exchanges.

Much Remains to Be Done

Many substantive differences can be addressed only through the voluntary efforts of foreign and domestic companies and their respective governments. For illustration, let us describe briefly some features of a company's annual reporting practice:

The overall report is issued in two publications: "Annual Report 1987 Philips" and "Financial Statements 1987 Philips." Included are two types of valuations—current value and historical cost—and two currency translations—into U.S. dollars and ECU (European Currency Unit). In the presentations based on historical costs, calculations are "substantially" in conformity with GAAP. The report also includes a "Notice to holders of shares of New York Registry," referring to Form 20-F filed with the SEC.

The company's report contains a section on the proposed distribution of income. A portion is retained, "with due observance of the provisions relating to legally required reserves. The remaining portion...is at the disposal of the General Meeting of Shareholders," except for the interim dividend payments, which do not require prior approval by the shareholders.

As stated or implied above, comparability of financial reporting has many implications. Here is an illustrative example of the far-reaching consequences of the competitive inequalities caused or aggravated by the lack of comparable rules and regulations:

In the United States, the requirement to amortize goodwill decreases a company's earnings. Moreover, the amortization is not deductible for tax purposes. In many other countries, goodwill is treated as an asset or, if amortized, as a tax-deductible expense. In either case, a foreign bidder trying to take over a U.S. company has a built-in competitive advantage.

Similar competitive inequalities may be found even within a single country such as the United States. A well-known case is the tax advantage of leveraged financing over equity financing, which is an important factor in favor of LBOs. The potentially adverse market impact of LBOs on company bondholders represents still another consequence that is neither predictable nor desirable.

Ethics Implications

Several observations seem pertinent, not only to the subject of intercountry relations but also partly to the domestic circumstances.

1. Integrity of the corporate disclosure system is conditioned by the general legal framework, industry tradition, community needs, and various other external factors, such as "stakeholders" and constituencies, market share, creditors, customers, competitors, and suppliers.
2. The prevailing traditional values and behavioral patterns, as reflected in corporate cultures, account for much of the diversity among the countries or among the domestic corporations.
3. Comparability of financial statements does not indicate necessarily that the related management actions, which influence the contents of those statements, are similarly comparable.
4. The increasing complexity of business ethics — the new and changing ethical dilemmas related to "nonmarket forces" such as an evergrowing variety of local, domestic, and foreign regulations and demands — may call for more political skills. It also may expose the executives acting as politicians, principally through lobbying, to the corresponding ethical risks.
5. Excessive conformism, in financial reporting as elsewhere, tends to create undue resistance. If successful, it often ends in a form-over-substance effect, despite its worthy goals and lofty rhetoric.

Chapter 9

Recommendations

Ethics in Business Practice

Individuals have to be able to define themselves in terms of ethics, as they understand and feel it, if they are to attain a state of mind that leads spontaneously to ethical behavior. Similarly, as organizations of people working together, companies ought to be able to define themselves in terms of ethics, if they are to attain a favorable ethical climate conducive to their overall success as business enterprises.

A company's performance, in an ethical sense and otherwise, depends on the presence of ethical individuals among its executives and other employees. In a favorable ethical climate, ethical behavior is encouraged and supported affirmatively. Company codes of ethics are suitable means of establishing and maintaining ethics-oriented organizational frameworks.

Corporate Codes of Ethics

If all activities in a company already are conducted at the desired level of ethics, a formal statement of the company's ethical standards is not necessary. Still, such a company might find it beneficial to adopt a code of ethics, if only to make the standards known to suppliers, contractors, and the public in general.

Individuals tend to see the world around them from their own perspective. As employees, they perceive company ethics primarily as manifested by the behavior of top executives rather than on the basis of what a company has issued in its code of ethics. To be effective, a company's code of ethics has to be supported by the practices of its leadership.

A code of ethics is a company's policy statement applicable to all

of its activities and relationships. It should identify principal responsibilities and commitments to all of its constituencies and to the
public. The main function of a company's code of ethics, however, is
to provide guidance and serve as an authoritative reference in cases
of ethical dilemmas.

Initial Steps Toward a Code of Ethics

Who takes the first step and why? The answers to the questions of
who and why have a significant bearing on how the work is done and
what its result will be.

In business enterprises, the initiative usually comes from the top.
Such an initiative has the best chance of developing and implementing
a company code of ethics quickly.

The same applies to evaluation of and changes in the existing code
of ethics. Such changes often directly address general public concern
about ethics and, as a consequence, give priority to the provisions
that will meet public expectations. As pointed out earlier, a majority
of the sample companies have codes of ethics that were developed
under similar circumstances in past years in response to the waves of
ethics-oriented general concerns or regulations.

It is our considered opinion that now is the time for more comprehensive efforts that will give full attention to all ethical aspects of
company activities and lead to a more favorable corporate ethical
climate.

Quite a few companies already have developed codes of ethics that
treat ethics as a company resource. It is likely that such an approach
also will satisfy all legitimate and realistic demands and expectations on the part of company constituencies and the general public as
well.

An initiative coming from someone other than a member of top
management preferably should include an outline of the basic policy
decisions to be made before such an effort is undertaken. It should
include convincing enough reasons or evidence to warrant serious
consideration by the corporate decision makers. Such an initiative
probably will come from company internal auditing in consultation
with the legal or personnel department, and the outline of the proposed
actions will be submitted first to the audit committee. At this stage,
it would be advisable to obtain support from the company's board of
directors. It is necessary, however, that the CEO accept the proposal
and authorize further action.

We already have covered several examples of the ethics programs instituted and implemented by some of the research sample companies. These programs will make it easier for employees to understand the standards and will establish appropriate procedures to monitor compliance. We have not found much information on any preliminary work in preparing a code of ethics or in reviewing an old one.

The next section presents preliminary considerations of various common questions and issues, as well as criteria for their treatment in standards of ethics. These points are applicable to companies of all sizes whose managements feel that the time has come to take a fresh look at the ethical side of their business endeavors. We have outlined these considerations as additional reference material for persons working on a company code of ethics.

Much more information on this subject is readily available from numerous sources, including expert consultants and collections of company codes. Numerous references to company views, statements, and codes of ethics can be found in Chapters 4 to 6 of this report, and Appendices A to C contain a selection of recently published reports and articles.

Preparing a Code of Ethics: Preliminary Considerations

Code of Ethics vs. Other Policies

Every major company and most of the mid-size companies already have a number of ethics-related provisions within their policies and procedures, although such provisions are not necessarily called "ethical" or separated from other provisions or items. Collectively, they represent the ethical side of the company as reflected in the current written materials.

Standards of business conduct stated separately as a company policy or set of policies preferably are issued in the form of a brochure for handy reference. A code of ethics is not simply one of the policies, for it applies to all other policies.

The code of ethics provides a frame of reference for application of other policies. To the extent that other policies refer to ethics or contain ethics-related provisions, those references or provisions are subject to interpretation in terms of the standards in the code of ethics.

The ethical side of the company policies, whether stated or implied, may differ among the policies. Standards set forth in the corporate code of ethics, on the other hand, state the basic policies and aspirations of the corporation in order to communicate the consensus on corporate ethics. An important goal is to instill a sense of ethics at the desired level throughout the corporation.

Ethics Consensus

A useful preliminary step in preparing a code of ethics is to take an inventory of the existing policies, statements, manuals, and other similar materials and to review and evaluate them as to ethics. The report on the findings will give an idea of the current status of ethics in the corporation as embodied in its practice-oriented materials. It will serve the immediate purpose of establishing a point of departure for developing the standards of business conduct in the code of ethics. It also will serve as a convenient reference for eliminating any discrepancies among the policies and for deciding on the changes or modifications needed to make all of them consistent with the new standards.

The new standards should uphold and strengthen the best among the "shared values" within the company. Some of those values, beliefs, or principles may not have been stated in any of the inventoried items, but they are part of the company's ethos and should be recognized in the new standards.

The next step is to review all applicable laws and regulations, considering their inherent ethical implications, locating references to ethics or related concepts, such as fairness, and identifying the corresponding ethical exposure of the company. A crucial set of decisions will have to be made at some point — how to formulate references to the law within the code of ethics.

Consistency

Consistency in itself is a component of ethics, one of the structural attributes of a code of ethics. The lack of consistency would create unfair situations by setting different standards for otherwise identical ethical questions. Perhaps even worse, it could make several standards applicable. Thus, one would face new ethical dilemmas as to the appropriate choice among the multiple ways of resolving a problem, all acceptable in terms of one or another of the standards or their interpretations.

The impact of varying conditions or circumstances is a valid concern;

only certain activities may be affected. Recognition of those factors is not in conflict with consistency. If the circumstances are expected to vary substantially, separate standards should be established within a subject or problem area.

One example is management accounting. The reports prepared for specific decisions or budgeting are not necessarily treated in conformity with generally accepted accounting principles. Instead of uniformity and completeness, the guiding concerns are appropriateness and selectivity, both in form and content. This is not in conflict with integrity of financial statements, but it preferably should be recognized under a separate standard.

Applicability

One aspect of applicability is to preserve consistency by observing certain distinctions among the standards. The core standards are uniformly applicable to all employees throughout the company. The specific standards should treat the varying degrees of relevance and areas of applicability adequately. Without specific standards, the core standards would have to be interpreted according to the situational factors, requirements, and conditions, with reference to the applicable laws, regulations, or company policies.

The extreme case, a code of ethics with only a few core standards, has a merely rhetorical role. It could not be used to identify or resolve ethical dilemmas.

The issue of applicability also is related to the degrees of enforcement. Some standards are mandatory, while some are applicable only to a certain extent or to certain types of ethical dilemmas. For example, political contributions by the company are prohibited, but this does not apply to contributions made by the employees themselves. Another example is the gradation of conflicts of interest — from the prohibited to the acceptable, subject to certain limits or disclosure and/or approval requirements.

Due to the mandatory nature of the law, applicability is not an issue subject to corporate standards of conduct. Compliance could be primarily a company responsibility or primarily affect an employee. In either case, however, there is an individual responsibility. The financial side of such problems, such as the indemnification of directors and officers to the extent permitted by applicable law, usually is covered in a separate corporate policy or in the certificate of incorporation and/or the bylaws.

Possible Problems

In principle, a code of ethics should give an uplifting flavor with the emphasis on the right action and the most ethical way of doing it. In practice, however, it is often simpler and more comprehensible to concentrate on possible problems. Take, for example, honesty and candor in all activities. They are essential, but it is almost equally important to know that by adhering to this highly ethical principle, employees may say something that will be harmful to the company or even illegal. An employee inadvertently may make unauthorized disclosures that could be used by a competitor or by someone who is considering the purchase or sale of company shares, and neither of those is necessarily the person whom the employee was talking with. It is, therefore, more effective and much safer to observe a "no" standard: Do not talk about the company.

Whatever an employee does or says in connection with his or her company may create a problem, unless the employee can do it or say it so that it does not have any negative or unlawful consequence. This is of essence in a code of ethics. The standards of conduct help employees recognize the instances of possible ethical dilemmas and guide them in the right direction.

Of special value in a code of ethics are the provisions that enable every employee to seek counsel — which minimizes exposure to ethical dilemmas — and to ask for assistance and protection from situational pressures involving ethical risks, such as following ethically questionable orders on the job.

From a company point of view, any activity may give rise to unethical behavior. It is crucial to identify the particularly sensitive areas that create relatively frequent or potentially serious ethical exposure.

Specific policies and procedures are often the best way of treating the main company activities, given adequate overall managerial and internal controls and proper security mechanisms. The task is to restrict the code of ethics to the topics that cannot be incorporated appropriately elsewhere, especially the matters everyone should know about.

Implementation and Compliance

Codes of ethics should be clear and simple so they can be implemented effectively and should include provision for disciplinary actions in case of violations. They should not contain nor imply anything beyond reasonable requirements or beyond the company's legitimate interests or its capacity to take appropriate actions.

General compliance matters should be covered, including the assurance that an employee's questions or reports regarding anyone's improper behavior will be held in strict confidence and that, as deemed necessary, other measures will be taken to protect the employee from any adverse consequences. Nothing should be stated without the benefit of a thorough review regarding the potential legal implications.

A well-designed and properly administered code of ethics loses much of its value if it does not reduce ethical dilemmas and incidents of unethical behavior. An ineffective treatment of the key topics, hard to understand and follow or difficult to administer, is in itself ethically questionable. Such a treatment is likely to happen when a code of ethics is developed primarily either as a control instrument or as a public relations device.

A code of ethics should be based on an impartial analysis of the existing state of ethics in a company and should reflect the behavior of its ethical employees. On the other hand, a favorable ethical climate cannot be created merely by adopting the views of those who would like to use the code as a pretext to impose their own values on everyone else. Even when they act with the best of intentions, the resulting standards may be biased or unrealistic. Not infrequently, an atmosphere unduly affected by certain dominant personalities and their ambitions may come to be resented by the deeply ethical individuals whose influence on others through their own behavior represents the backbone of the company's ethical well-being.

It is in the spirit of the discussion presented above — in this section and elsewhere in the report — that we have drafted a set of core standards for codes of ethics. The draft was distributed for review and comment to 20 companies. The final version appears in Figure 20.

Figure 20
Core Standards for Company Codes of Ethics

Preamble: This set of standards constitutes the Company's Code of Ethics (Code), which represents our current ethical consensus regarding the maintainable ethical level of business conduct, as ascertained and approved by the Board of Directors. Some of the standards supplement ethics-related provisions of various Company policies and procedures, but the standards take precedence in matters

Figure 20 (continued)

of interpretation and compliance. Changes in the Code are to be recommended exclusively by the Audit Committee.

No employee, regardless of position or function in the Company, is allowed to tamper with or to downgrade the significance of any standard, either explicitly or implicitly, by his or her behavior. In case of doubt as to proper application of a standard, written opinion of the Legal Department can be obtained.

Standard 1: It is the policy of the Company to comply strictly in all respects with all applicable laws and regulations. Diligent observance of the law is a requirement from which there can be no exception. Supervisors must make sure that all applicable laws are known by them and by the personnel under their supervision.

Standard 2: It is the overall policy of the Company to organize and carry out its activities toward the goal of a sustainable successful performance in the best interest of shareholders and other constituencies, with an overriding concern for observance of the highest ethical principles as they apply to business policies and practices.

Standard 3: The Company will promote fair competition and candid treatment of its customers or clients. Integrity of information communicated in soliciting business or in marketing products and services is the obligation of all those involved in such efforts, including company-authorized nonemployee representatives, dealers, and contractors. No one is authorized to make a promise or commitment that the company cannot or does not intend to meet.

Standard 4: The Company will always act honorably toward those who do business with the Company or are otherwise parties in a mutual relationship with the Company.

Standard 5: The Company is committed to support and contribute to the efforts undertaken in public interest, especially those affecting its community, its employees, its industry, or business at large. The Company will not participate, directly or indirectly, in any program or activity where the company role is not or appears not to be ethically sound.

Standard 6: The Company's continued success and good reputation depend on a consistently reliable high-quality performance of its employees in every situation and under all circumstances. Every employee should have the working knowledge and competence needed to achieve and maintain satisfactory performance. No employee should knowingly be given an assignment involving unwarranted ethical, physical, or professional risks.

Figure 20 (continued)

Standard 7: Every supervisor's task is to create and maintain an on-the-job atmosphere conducive to self-esteem and care about the job and other employees, and an experience-based confidence on the part of the employees that good performance is given due recognition.

Standard 8: Employees are expected to uphold the spirit as well as the letter of the Code and be guided by the Code in all business dealings and relationships—toward one another, with government, shareholders, customers, suppliers, competitors, community, and everyone else affected by their behavior or performance in any way or to any degree.

Standard 9: The Company's property encompasses monetary values reflected in the Company's records as well as any other tangible or intangible items, rights, or claims whose loss would diminish the Company's value or adversely affect its earning potential. Every employee shall safeguard the Company's property. No misappropriation, neglect, or waste is to be tolerated. No employee is entitled to use the Company property in ways not intended to serve the Company's legitimate interests.

Standard 10: Every employee is subject to complete, accurate, and timely financial accountability and/or reporting requirements as needed to assure the integrity of the Company's accounting records, financial statements, and disclosures. This includes candid cooperation with auditors, internal and external.

In particular, with respect to the Company's accounting records, employees will not knowingly:

(a) make or cause to be made any false, artificial, or misleading entry that does not accurately and properly record, in accordance with supporting facts or documents, a transaction, acquisition, or disposition of assets.

(b) fail to make or cause another person to fail to make any entry necessary to make the Company's accounting records accurate and fairly reflecting transactions, acquisitions, or dispositions of assets, or tamper with the integrity of financial reporting by making or causing another person to make false or misleading statements in presenting or interpreting the Company's performance or financial condition.

Standard 11: Any information developed or acquired by the Company is proprietary and should be safeguarded and used, like any other Company property, solely for the proper conduct of the Company's business.

Figure 20 (continued)

All information pertaining to the Company's business that an employee obtains in the course of his or her employment is confidential unless the Company has made such information public. Unauthorized disclosure is prohibited.

Any employee who is uncertain whether something is confidential should presume that it is. No employee should attempt to obtain confidential information that does not relate to his or her employment duties.

Standard 12: The payment of normal discounts and allowances, commissions, and fees and the extension of customary courtesies in the ordinary course of business are permissible, provided that they are: (1) reasonable in nature, frequency, and amount and consistent with applicable laws, and (2) properly recorded and of sufficiently limited value so they cannot be construed as bribes, payoffs, or kickbacks or as having the purpose to influence the recipients to give favored treatment to the Company's business.

Standard 13: All employees are to be treated equitably. This is a general responsibility of the Company's Chief Executive Officer. No employee is to be treated arbitrarily in a materially different way from other comparable employees. No employee should be subject to exemplary punishment, and no employee who has committed a serious violation is to be granted immunity from the enforcement of this Code.

Standard 14: This Code is not intended to impose any burdensome requirements on the personal affairs of the employees. Every employee should ensure that there is no real or apparent conflict between his or her interests and the Company's interests. Any employee having an interest or relationship requiring disclosure under the Company's conflict-of-interest policy, as currently in effect, has an affirmative duty to comply with its provisions.

Standard 15: All employees are encouraged to seek advice of their immediate superiors. Any observed violations of the Code are to be reported—through their superiors or directly to the person designated by the Company.

The Company will protect from any harmful consequences all employees who act in good faith either to comply or to assure or promote compliance with this Code.

Standard 16: Except for the protection clause in Standard 15, this Code does not constitute or grant a legal right of any nature to anyone in the Company and no standard is to be interpreted to have conferred any kinds of rights or privileges upon any employee or group of employees.

Preparing a Code of Ethics: Actions and Procedures

Introductory Actions by the CEO

The CEO must first issue initial instructions about drafting a statement of the basic company views, to serve as a general framework for the work of preparing the code of ethics. This statement can be prepared by a task force formed to carry out the work or by someone else who was given this assignment before the task force was appointed by the CEO.

It is preferable to have a small task force. It should include employees of varying backgrounds, however. No direct participation by a senior executive is necessary, but an executive should be given overseeing responsibility and authority to request cooperation of all employees with the task force.

The CEO then announces the program in a memorandum or similar means that will communicate the nature and purpose of the work to be done. The announcement should contain the names and positions of the task force responsible for this work, including the name of the executive in charge. The employees should be instructed that their cooperation in this effort is essential and, preferably, the CEO should explain what their cooperation may involve and why it will be necessary for the task force to contact various departments and individuals for information and consulting purposes. Finally, the CEO should encourage the employees to give their own views or questions to an easily accessible member of the task force, whose name and phone number should be identified in the announcement.

Task Force Program

The task force should prepare a detailed program with a time schedule for completion of every major phase in the course of its activities. The work requiring contributions from other people should be scheduled in consultation with each individual and his or her supervisor. The program of task force activities may include meetings or discussion sessions — departmental or with groups of work teams in various locations.

A sufficient degree of flexibility is an important feature of a realistic program of action. An allowance for logistical or other possible problems and delays should be an explicit part of the overall time schedule.

Employee Meetings

We recommend that the task force program provide for attendance by at least one of its members at all meetings held on ethics. We also recommend that for each of these meetings a list of questions and answers be prepared. The answers preferably should be given in a tentative manner or provide a choice of applicable alternatives, all of which are considered acceptable but not equally desirable. Or the alternatives may differ in some other way, for example, in their possible consequences, which are not necessarily ascertainable at the time an ethical dilemma has to be resolved. The main reasons for the above recommendations on preparation of meeting materials are:

1. Custom-made questions and answers can focus on specific concerns of the particular group of employees. As a matter of fact, those groups should be as homogeneous as possible with respect to the ethical side of their regular duties and work assignments. Members of such groups tend to participate more freely and openly in discussions. It is also a good idea to: (a) distribute the question-and-answer sets ahead of the scheduled meeting time, and (b) stress in the meeting announcement that the task force will welcome additional materials developed by any individual invited to the meeting and either submitted to the task force or presented at the meeting.

2. A similar approach can be used, especially in smaller companies, by scheduling discussion meetings to follow the completion of each major portion of the code of ethics, as drafted by the task force. The question-and-answer sets then can focus on the completed part of the draft. Copies of the draft should be distributed with the questions and answers and brief explanations of the respective standards.

3. Carefully organized meetings of well-informed employees offer several advantages: (a) the structure of the pre-meeting process is conducive to active participation in the meeting discussion, (b) it is possible to conduct meetings at a higher communication level, (c) open-ended and alternative-answer formulation of certain discussion topics stimulates ideas, and (d) each meeting can be less time-consuming and its purposes can be accomplished more effectively.

Finally, we recommend that the discussion leader be someone other than the individual who attends the meeting on behalf of the task force. The task force member or delegated representative of the task force should be an active observer. This primary role could be complemented by having the task force member add to the discussion as needed and appropriate, so as to clarify certain positions taken by the task force on specific issues or with respect to the general policy. If several meetings of the same group are to be held, the role of discussion leader should be rotated, so that the discussion leader is always the person most suitable for the particular meeting.

After every meeting, a set of notes prepared by the task force member in attendance should be presented for review and discussion by the task force. Any action affecting the matters discussed at a meeting and taken as a consequence of the discussion should be communicated to those who attended that meeting.

The executive in charge from time to time may inform the audit committee and the CEO of the meetings and the resulting actions. Such briefings preferably should be separate from the task force progress reports. The purpose of the briefings is to show the interactive and cooperative effects of the task force efforts.

Initial Monitoring

It is advisable for the executive in charge of the work of preparing a code of ethics subsequently to assume the role of chief ethics officer or serve as the liaison officer, at least during the initial period of implementation. In any case, the length of the initial implementation period should be one of the task force recommendations. Such a recommendation also may include an outline of the interim monitoring system, which may be modified after an evaluation at the end of the initial implementation period.

It is likely that a well-prepared and implemented code of ethics will allow company management to simplify the initial monitoring system. If this is not the case, company management may decide to simplify the code of ethics as well.

Excessive Implementation Requirements

If implementation of the code of ethics requires extensive or complex monitoring of compliance it probably means that the code is defective. An effective code, as a rule, lifts the ethical climate to a higher level that, in turn, creates favorable conditions so there is less need for and dependence on monitoring and control mechanisms.

In any case, ethics maintenance is a cost to a company. The

constructive uplifting effects associated with a code of ethics should exceed this cost by a noticeable margin. Otherwise, ethics maintenance on the basis of a code of ethics becomes an avoidable expense. This is not meant to imply that ethics as such is not a valuable company resource, regardless of the relative value of having it stated in the form of a code of ethics.

Inadequate Implementation

Potentially the worst situation would be created by reducing a code of ethics to what we called earlier "the dormant observation" status. In such a case, the mere existence of a company code of ethics has a misleading and possibly damaging impact on the ethical climate, though the code of ethics may continue to be useful for publicity and similar purposes.

Adherence to standards of ethics incorporated in the corporate culture is not as essential as it is when those standards are issued in a code of ethics. Corporate culture of a company also may become just an abstraction, not really representing the company practice or having any appreciable impact. Such a situation would not necessarily create significant ethical problems. This is yet another important difference between a code of ethics and a corporate culture, though a company professing to have a corporate culture, while not practicing it, may be ethically better off without its corporate culture pronouncements.

Other Recommendations

Core Standards

Figure 20 suggests a set of core standards that cover topics applicable to a wide range of companies. We recommend that each core standard be considered for inclusion in a corporate code of ethics.

Some of the core standards have not been found in any code of ethics reviewed in the course of our study. On the other hand, several topics prominent in many codes of ethics, often covered in a series of related standards, are condensed here to a single core standard or do not appear at all.

In our opinion, each core standard is clear as to its meaning and intended role within the code. Nevertheless, it is feasible to accomplish the same purposes through abbreviated versions of some core standards.

A few standards may be omitted without any serious effect on the completeness of coverage in a corporate code. It is more likely, however, that some matters of significant ethical concern to certain companies are not covered or not sufficiently covered in these core standards, so expanded versions of the standards or inclusion of additional standards will be necessary.

Steps Toward a Simpler Code

Standard 3: Leave out the second sentence.
Standard 6: Omit the first sentence.
Standard 8: Shorten by leaving out all text after "relationships."
Standard 9: Leave out the first sentence and the fourth one.
Standard 10: Keep the first paragraph. Leave out the rest.
Standard 11: Omit the standard or reduce it to the first two paragraphs.
Standard 12: Omit. This topic can be covered in the conflict-of-interest policy.
Standard 13: Omit.
Standard 16: Omit.

The above changes and omissions would reduce the total size of six standards by more than one-half their length and reduce the code from 16 to 12.

Additional Standards

Due to the diversity of company needs and views, it is not practicable to present a comprehensive list of topics that might require expansion of individual core standards or inclusion of additional ones. We also have to keep in mind space constraints and the limited scope of the information sources used. Hence, we will restrict our list of additional topics to some examples:

1. *Antitrust Laws.* In principle, all applicable laws and regulations are covered in Standard 1. Direct references to fair competition and conduct toward company competitors are made in Standards 3 and 8, respectively. A company having a particular exposure to activities that could involve violations of antitrust laws may want to add some specific coverage in its code of ethics.

2. *Transactions with U.S. Government.* Defense contractors should address this topic in their codes of ethics (see Appendix A).

3. *Equal Employment Opportunity and Affirmative Action.* Standard 13 refers to this area of company commitment and responsibility. A more explicit treatment might be warranted in some companies.
4. *Conflicts of Interest.* Standard 14 refers to a separate conflict-of-interest policy. In Chapter 6, the section titled Policies on Conflicts of Interest gives detailed coverage of this subject.
5. *Community, Political, and Charitable Contributions.* Standards 5 and 12 address this area. Some other aspects, such as using substantial time during working hours, preferably should be dealt with in the conflict-of-interest policy. The same applies to various outside positions and activities of company employees.

The above list appears separately from the list of steps toward a simpler code, but in practice, the two types of adaptation may be undertaken simultaneously. The need to accommodate additional standards may, in fact, provide an extra incentive to eliminate some of the core standards so as to keep the code within the desired overall length.

Initial Implementation Program

The code is issued preferably as a brochure with three attachments: (1) an acknowledgement form to be signed and filed by the date designated on the form, (2) a set of questions and answers, and (3) conflict-of-interest materials, comprising the policy and the respective forms.

Copies of the code and its attachments should be distributed to all employees, along with an announcement by the CEO. All outstanding company policies and procedures should have been reviewed during the preliminary work on preparing the code of ethics, and all such materials should be re-evaluated on the basis of the final edition of the code. Special attention should be given to any ethics-related provisions outside the code. The goal is the highest possible conformity with the standards in the code.

The code presented earlier states that its standards take precedence in matters of interpretation and compliance. It is not a recommended practice to rely on this provision instead of taking immediate action, if any is needed, to minimize possible future controversies or conflicts.

Similarly, the initial implementation program should cover materials issued elsewhere that are used in the company or that may affect ethical behavior of any employees, such as professional codes of ethics.

Again, if any action is called for, it should be taken as part of the initial implementation of the code. The same applies to policies and procedures issued by company subsidiaries, unless they have been included as part of the work related to other company materials.

Compliance

During the initial implementation period, monitoring of compliance should be a responsibility of the executive who was in charge of the task force that drafted the code of ethics. This executive also should be in charge of the work on preparing a proposal for simplifying the monitoring system after the initial implementation period. If feasible, he or she also then should remain in charge of the regular monitoring system.

How is monitoring organized and maintained? A general answer would be that this type of monitoring does not have to be significantly different from monitoring company performances in other respects, such as quality control. Several specific methods seem to be suitable:

1. Using a testing procedure to collect a sample of recent actions or decisions that could have involved ethical dilemmas, to be reviewed carefully from an ethical point of view. The method of sample selection should vary in terms of locations, types of decisions, and the hierarchical level at which decisions were made. The experience based on the testing results should be used to modify this method of analysis or to replace the testing by some other procedure.

2. Analyzing compliance with respect to one or more standards of the code, particularly those covering especially sensitive areas where the ethical exposure is relatively high or areas in which some symptoms of possible noncompliance have been observed or even reported.

3. Reviewing all violations, especially those that may indicate a degree of neglect, indifference, or collusion.

4. Holding occasional informal discussions with individuals at various management levels regardless of their work performance records in order to ascertain their managerial style.

In most companies, it will be sufficient to assign the monitoring task to one person, who should be given direct access to the audit committee or who will be authorized to submit reports directly to the ethics committee, if such a committee is formed to oversee compliance. It would seem practical to include monitoring as one of the responsibilities of the employees who already have direct access to the audit committee, such as internal auditors.

In the process of selecting the appropriate person or persons for the monitoring of compliance, it is important to keep in mind that monitoring ethics is different in many respects from company controls performed by internal auditors. The principal tasks of monitoring ethics are to identify and use the most constructive means of raising the level of the ethical climate and to minimize ethical risks. The search for cases of noncompliance is of secondary importance. In the area of ethics, proper motivation of employees and recognition of their on-the-job problems caused by undue exposure to ethical risks are often sufficient to assure a high degree of compliance.

The person in charge of monitoring should not be engaged directly in the process of investigating serious violations. Taking the role of an adversary is not entirely compatible with the advisory image the person in charge of monitoring should cultivate. His or her role is closer to that of an ombudsman than a detective or prosecutor.

Management should avoid any hasty actions that could be interpreted as or have the appearance of being discriminatory or premature. No information should be disclosed to or discussed with anyone not directly engaged in the investigation. The suspected employee is not to be contacted or notified until a decision has been made to activate the company's disciplinary proceedings, in consultation with a legal expert.

Any employee charged with a violation of the company's code of ethics should be afforded ample opportunity to explain his or her actions before the disciplinary action is taken and, upon request, should be allowed to appeal to the audit committee. Disciplinary actions are taken as appropriate, applying principles of fairness. Details of such matters should be specified in personnel policies and procedures.

Except in cases of unlawful behavior, any attempted explanation saying that "everyone else is doing it" should not be dismissed summarily as an irrelevant excuse. Any such allegation should be investigated. All enforcement activities should be conducted with a view toward improvement of the overall ethical conditions in the company.

The monitors should pay close attention to managerial actions that help create or maintain situational pressures adverse to ethical behavior. Certain managerial styles may contribute to noncompliance, for example, habitual acceptance of success, of things that work, and refraining from asking any "critical" questions. A similar situation is a manager's inclination to get overly impatient with a scrupulous employee who "asks too many questions" or who differs in any way from those who simply act as loyal team players. Ethically sound managerial style may not be always in the best interest of every manager. It is the job of ethics monitoring to see to it that such conflicting considerations are reconciled in a way that gives ethics the upper hand.

Periodic compliance reports are summarized for the CEO and the audit committee, unless they want to see certain individual reports such as those involving a designated flaw or all individual reports on upper-level executives. It is recommended that all matters related to ethics be taken under consideration by the company once a year as a regular practice.

Appendix A

Reports of the Commissions

Appendix A-1 — A Quest for Excellence[1]
Final Report to the President, June 1986

In July 1985, President Reagan established the President's Blue Ribbon Commission on Defense Management, chaired by David Packard, to conduct a defense management study and report its findings and recommendations. The body of the Final Report contains four chapters: (1) National Security Planning and Budgeting, (2) Military Organization and Command, (3) Acquisition, Organization and Procedures, and (4) Government-Industry Accountability.

In his Foreword, Chairman Packard stresses the need for "centers of management excellence" — giving a few capable people the authority and responsibility to do their job, maintaining short lines of communication, and holding people accountable for results.

The Final Report contains a summary of the report and the Commission's findings and recommendations. The recommendations also are set forth in more detail as Appendix A. All appended materials are included in a separately issued Appendix to Final Report.

Codes of Conduct for Defense Contractors

In Chapter 4, under II-A, "Contractor Standards of Conduct" (p. 81), the Commission recommends that:

Defense contractors must promulgate and enforce codes of conduct that address their unique problems.

---

[1]Summary review notes and selected excerpts.

The Commission's specific recommendations, on pp. 83-84, are presented here in an abbreviated version:

1. Written standards of ethical business conduct should include: (a) procedures for employees to report apparent misconduct, and (b) procedures for protecting employees who report instances of apparent misconduct.

2. Codes of conduct should address conflicts of interest that might arise in conducting negotiations for future employment with employees of the Department of Defense and in hiring or assigning responsibilities to former DoD officials.

3. Each contractor should distribute copies of its standards of ethical business conduct to all employees at least annually and to new employees when hired. Review of standards and typical business situations that require ethical judgments should be a regular part of an employee's work experience and performance evaluations.

4. Responsibility to oversee monitoring and enforcement of compliance should be vested, at least by major contractors, in their audit committees consisting entirely of nonemployee members of their boards of directors. Suitable alternative mechanisms should be developed where it is not feasible for a contractor to establish such a committee.

"The Commission believes that *self*-governance is the most promising mechanism to foster improved contract compliance....The extent of each contractor's efforts in doing so will reflect the level of reputation for integrity it intends to set for itself." (p. 84)

Contractor Internal Auditing

The Final Report addresses the subject of contractor internal auditing on pp. 85-89. The following two points seem particularly relevant here: (1) compliance with the contractor's standards of ethical conduct should be covered by the design of internal control, and (2) internal auditors should not report to any manager with direct responsibility for the subject of an audit — there should be sufficient direct reporting channels to the independent audit committee.

Department of Defense Standards of Conduct

The following excerpts highlight the Commission's approach and reasoning:

1. Vigorous administration of current ethics regulations for military and civilian personnel to assure that its employees comply with the same high standards expected of contractor personnel. This effort should include development of specific ethics guidance and specialized training programs, including post-government relationships with defense contractors (the "revolving door" phenomenon).

2. Ethical standards are only as easy to observe, administer, and enforce as they are certain in scope, simple in concept, and clear in application. Undue complexity and vagueness — for example, that we believe characterizes current financial disclosure reporting requirements — serve no legitimate public purpose. Either can transform ethical standards from matters of principle to mere traps for the unwary,...

Appendix A-2 — A Quest for Excellence
Appendix to the Final Report

Sixteen items appear in this separate volume. With respect to ethics, the Final Report (see Appendix A-1) makes several references to:
- "Defense Industry Initiatives on Business Ethics and Conduct," and
- Ethics Resource Center, "Final Report and Recommendations on Voluntary Corporate Policies, Practices, and Procedures Relating to Ethical Business Conduct" (1986).

Initiatives

Titled "Business Ethics and Conduct," this document contains: I. Principles, II. Implementation: Supporting Programs, and Questionnaire. The Final Report refers to it on p. 78 and states that the document was "signed to date by at least 32 major defense contractors...."

The introductory paragraphs are quoted below:

> The defense industry companies who sign this document already have, or commit to adopt and implement, a set of principles of business ethics and conduct that acknowledge and address their corporate responsibilities under federal procurement laws and to the public. Further, they accept the responsibility to create an environment in which compliance with federal procurement laws and free, open, and timely reporting of violations become the felt responsibility of every employee in the defense industry.
>
> In addition to adopting and adhering to this set of six principles of business ethics and conduct, we will take the leadership in making the principles a standard for the entire defense industry.

The second part, on Implementation, deals individually with each of the six principles stated in the first part. The concluding section, Questionnaire, contains 18 items. As stated under Principle 6: Public Accountability, the questionnaire is to be completed by the company's external auditors or "similar independent organization" and submitted annually to "an external independent body which will report the results for the industry as a whole and release the data simultaneously to the companies and the general public." (p. 44)

The above is apparently designed as a consequence of the serious concern of the Commission as reflected in the Final Report. Among the data cited is the information that the Department of Defense "annually conducts business with some 60,000 prime contractors and hundreds of thousands of other suppliers and subcontractors." (p. 75)

Voluntary Actions

The Ethics Resource Center's work for the Commission was a major source of the information regarding codes of conduct for defense contractors. The Center's report and recommendations are presented briefly on p. 82 of the Final Report.

The Center's survey for the Commission found that 73% of respondent defense contractors had adopted written standards of conduct or codes of ethics by 1979. This is comparable to the record of American firms in general. According to research sponsored by the Ethics Resource Center in 1979, 73% of the 650 largest U.S. corporations had written standards or codes. In the meantime, however, the situation has changed in terms of the relative percentages. The Center's survey (1985) for the Commission shows an increase from 73% to 92% for the respondent defense contractors, while the Bentley College Survey

(1985) found virtually no change since 1979 among 279 major corporations (74.6% in 1985 vs. 73% in 1979).

Appendix A-3 — Report of the National Commission on Fraudulent Financial Reporting, October 1987

The six-member National Commission on Fraudulent Financial Reporting, chaired by James C. Treadway, Jr., was a private-sector initiative, jointly sponsored and funded by the American Institute of Certified Public Accountants (AICPA), the American Accounting Association (AAA), the Financial Executives Institute (FEI), the Institute of Internal Auditors (IIA), and the National Association of Accountants (NAA). The same five sponsors later established the Implementation Oversight Committee. The NAA is very active in the implementation effort.

From October 1985 to September 1987, the Commission studied the financial reporting system in the United States. The mission was to identify causal factors that can lead to fraudulent financial reporting and steps to reduce its incidence.

The Commission's report focuses on public companies. "The term public company generally includes companies owned by public investors." This was interpreted to include public companies that report to the Securities and Exchange Commission (SEC), as well as certain financial institutions that are subject to the disclosure provisions of the federal securities laws, and certain mutual thrift institutions.

The body of the Commission's report contains five chapters:

1. Overview of the Financial Reporting System and Fraudulent Financial Reporting
2. Recommendations for the Public Company
3. Recommendations for the Independent Public Accountant
4. Recommendations for the SEC and Others to Improve the Regulatory and Legal Environment
5. Recommendations for Education

Overview

The Commission's findings relate occurrences of fraud to the impact of certain environmental, institutional, or individual forces and opportunities. The analysis of causes of fraudulent financial reporting, which includes examples of situational pressures and fraud opportunities, concludes with the following paragraph on p. 24:

> A weak corporate ethical climate exacerbates these situations. Opportunities for fraudulent financial reporting also increase dramatically when the accounting principles for transactions are nonexistent, evolving, or subject to varying interpretations.

The perpetrators of fraudulent financial reporting, often within a company's top management, use many different means, but "the effect of their actions is almost always to inflate or 'smooth' earnings or to overstate the company's assets." In many cases, fraudulent financial reporting is the culmination of a series of acts that, initially, may not be fraudulent. "When the tone set by top management permits or encourages such activities, eventually the result may be fraudulent financial reporting." (p. 24)

The Public Company

Recommendations for the public company are designed to reduce the incidence of fraudulent reporting by addressing the problem at two levels: (1) an appropriate tone by the top management, and (2) the effectiveness of the functions that are critical to the integrity of financial reporting.

In the section on the tone at the top, the Commission's recommended framework for the top management's actions includes three steps: identifying and understanding the factors that can lead to fraudulent financial reporting, assessing the respective risks, and maintaining internal controls that provide reasonable assurance that fraudulent financial reporting will be prevented or subject to early detection. The Commission then recommends that every public company develop and enforce a written code of corporate conduct "as a tangible embodiment of the tone at the top." (p. 32)

In the sections on the critical functions, the Commission addresses: accounting, internal audit, audit committee, and communications to financial statement users — Management Report and Audit Committee Chairman's Letter. The Commission then offers recommendations in connection with two specific areas for improvement: seeking a second opinion on a significant accounting issue, and the role of the audit committee in quarterly reporting. The chapter ends with the recommendation that the Commission's sponsoring organizations cooperate in developing additional integrated guidance on internal control.

The Commission's recommendation on codes of corporate conduct is given below as it appears on p. 35 of the Commission's report:

> *Recommendation:* Public companies should develop and enforce written codes of corporate conduct. Codes of conduct should foster a strong ethical climate and open channels of communication to help protect against fraudulent financial reporting. As a part of its ongoing oversight of the effectiveness of internal controls, a company's audit committee should review annually the program that management establishes to monitor compliance with the code.

The text that amplifies and explains the Commission's recommendation on the codes of corporate conduct is condensed here from pp. 35-36:

> A strong corporate ethical climate, free flow of information, monitoring and enforcement are the key topics. There is a great deal of diversity in written codes of corporate conduct. Sufficient resources and the full support of management — the CEO in particular — are needed to develop a code tailored to the company's circumstances. An accessible complaint and appeal mechanism should be set, and the code "should protect employees who use these internal procedures against reprisal." (p. 36)

The Independent Public Accountant

The first recommendation calls for a restatement of the auditor's responsibility for detecting fraudulent financial reporting. In the related explanatory comments, the Commission stresses once again the importance of a strong corporate ethical climate. "The standards should require the auditor to assess the company's control environment, including its management, in planning the audit. The assumption of management integrity is one of the key areas where guidance should be changed." (p. 51)

Other recommendations are described briefly below:

1. The Commission's recommendations would require: (a) greater use of analytical review procedures and (b) timely review of quarterly financial data.
2. Two recommendations are designed to strengthen the profession's quality assurance program with respect to: (a) the peer review and (b) review by a concurring or second partner. The third

recommendation highlights the tone at the top, which is as important as the tone set by top managements in public companies.

3. Finally, the Commission considers the impact of the CPA work on both the preparers and users of CPA reports: (a) two recommendations to strengthen communication with users, and (b) a recommendation "that the Auditing Standards Board (ASB) of the AICPA be reorganized to include equal representation and participation by knowledgeable representatives of the constituencies that have a significant interest in the financial reporting process." (p. 49)

The Regulatory and Legal Environment

Most of the 12 recommendations concern the SEC. Among the three "additional SEC enforcement remedies," the Commission recommends, "The SEC should seek explicit statutory authority to bar or suspend corporate officers and directors involved in fraudulent financial reporting from future service in that capacity in a public company." (p. 66)

Education

The Commission recommends curriculum-wide exposure to fraudulent financial reporting with more adequate coverage of the ethics of financial reporting. "The business and accounting curricula should emphasize ethical values by integrating their development with the acquisition of knowledge and skills to help prevent, detect, and deter fraudulent financial reporting." (p. 82) References to the subject of "ethical values" are incorporated in the Commission's specific recommendations as well — on faculty development and classroom materials, professional certification examinations, and continuing professional education.

Other

The Commission directed an extensive research program. In addition to the 10 external research studies, done by outside experts, the Commission's staff completed more than 20 research projects and briefing papers. "Significant findings of the research efforts are incorporated into the text of the report, and Appendices B and C summarize the research." (p. 3)

To supplement this research program, the Commission reviewed related studies and interviewed and consulted numerous experts. Appendices also include composite case studies (Harvard Business School), good practice guidelines, and other materials.

The Commission's recommendations are meant to be viewed as a unified set; they have been formulated "to work synergistically." (p. 7) Our descriptive compilation presented here is not intended to be representative of the Commission's report or its recommendations.

Research Reports

Appendix B-1

Corporate Ethics. Ronald E. Berenbeim. The Conference Board, New York, NY, 1987.

This research report, especially Chapters 1 and 2, mainly is based on the results of a mail questionnaire survey of 2,100 worldwide businesses. Responses to the Board's survey were received from 300 companies (252 U.S. and 48 non-U.S.). The questions and answers are displayed in tables and charts throughout the report.

Chapter 1 focuses on 27 business issues involving ethical considerations listed under four categories: equity (3 issues), rights (8 issues), honesty (8 issues), and exercise of corporate power (8 issues). As shown in Table 1 on p. 3, there is "widespread agreement" (80% or more say "yes") that the subject raised ethical questions for business on a total of seven issues from three categories: honesty (3), rights (3), and corporate power (1). In the "moderate level of agreement" group (50% - 79% say "yes") are issues such as: security of company records (76%), workplace safety (76%), product safety standards (74%), shareholder interest (68%), corporate due process (65%), plant/facility closures and downsizing (55%), and political action committees (55%). The bottom "no consensus" group (fewer than half say "yes") comprises four issues: social issues raised by religious organizations (47%), comparable worth (43%), product pricing (42%), and executive salaries (37%).

Although 76% of the respondents have a code of ethics, "there was little difference between the responses of companies with and without codes" (p. 3). U.S. and non-U.S. companies were in substantial accord on most issues. Plant closures, product safety, and comparable worth were of greater concern to the non-U.S. respondents, while employee health screening is regarded much more seriously by the U.S. respondents.

Chapter 2 presents responses to the questions derived from the four case studies and respective discussions given in full within the chapter: 1. Business Meeting or Vacation?, 2. Toxic Emission Standards and a "Whistle-Blower," 3. Acquisition and Layoff, and 4. Inside Information.

Two other sources were used in Chapter 3, in addition to the survey responses: 1. The Conference Board's Watson Research Collection, which includes 238 corporate codes of conduct, and 2. interviews and discussions with key participants in code drafting. The code drafting is featured in an illustration: "Drafting a Code: A Detailed Look at One Company's Experience." Materials from the same company also appear as Exhibits 1 and 2. All together, the report includes eight exhibits:

1. Security Pacific Corporation Statement of Corporate and Employee Commitments,
2. Security Pacific Model Questions and Answers for Discussion Leaders,
3. Pfizer Statement of Corporate Philosophy,
4. McDonnell Douglas Corporation Code of Ethics,
5. Nestle Profile,
6. JC Penney Hypothetical Situations and Analyses,
7. American Can Company (now Primerica Corp.) Corporate Conduct Questionnaire,
8. General Dynamics Ethics Program Organization.

It is evident that the questionnaire items were selected carefully and case studies were well prepared. The overall design, though relatively complex, accommodates a variety of materials with a great degree of internal balance and unity of purpose. It also has a bit of a conceptual flavor — enough to serve as an "anchor" set at the very beginning — perhaps more ambitious in design than as carried out.

Appendix B-2

Fraudulent and Questionable Financial Reporting, A Corporate Perspective. Kenneth A. Merchant. Financial Executives Research Foundation, Morristown, NJ, 1987.

This monograph covers the full spectrum of financial-reporting practices, from the clearly fraudulent ones to those instances where a degree of deception appears unintentional or almost unavoidable and the element of deceptiveness is hardly detectable. Several complementary sources and methods were used in the course of the research on which the monograph is based.

The search for examples of deceptive financial reporting included reviews of relevant literature and a study of complaints and recent court cases, supplemented by discussion with knowledgeable individuals. Interviews were conducted in six firms that had not been involved in recent cases of deceptive practices. Two case studies prepared by Joseph P. Mulloy under the direction of Kenneth A. Merchant were discussed by two panels recruited by the Financial Executives Research Foundation.

Copies of the case studies can be obtained from the Harvard Business School. They also appear in *Report of the National Commission on Fraudulent Financial Reporting* (1987) as Appendix E.

In Chapter 5: Conclusion, the author demonstrates the scope of the problem area graphically (Figure 1) as "an acceptability continuum" from totally acceptable to totally unacceptable financial-reporting practices. As to the means of reducing exposure, the author concluded that "Absolute prescriptions...cannot be provided. Causes of deceptive practices are highly situational. In any given situation, if one control does not work, another might, or perhaps some combination of controls will work." (p. 43)

Appendix B-3

Ethics in American Business. Touche Ross & Co., January 1988.

This publication neatly presents the results of a mail questionnaire survey that covered eight questions. For each, there is an analytical breakdown of responses (Figures 1-8).

Altogether, 1,082 responses are included. They were received mostly from officers or directors of corporations. The questionnaires (total of 8,180) were mailed to: (1) directors and top executives of major corporations, (2) deans of business schools, and (3) U.S. senators and representatives.

For our purposes, the following statement (from the Introduction, p. 1) is of special interest:

Perhaps the most striking finding of the survey...is that a clear majority (63 percent) believe that a business enterprise actually strengthens its competitive position by maintaining high ethical standards....

From the 12 "other interesting findings" cited on pp. 1-2, let us quote the following two:

> Intense concentration on short-term earnings is a major threat to American business ethics today. Respondents rank this as almost equal to the threat posed by decay in cultural and social institutions.

> The adoption of business codes of ethics is the most effective way of encouraging ethical business behavior, respondents believe. The least effective way is legislation.

Appendix B-4

Corporate Ethics: A Prime Business Asset. The Business Round-table, February 1988.

Labeled on the cover as, "A Report on Policy and Practice in Company Conduct," this book is the third work in the area of corporate responsibility and ethics issued by The Business Roundtable since its founding in 1972. The earlier two are a report on business conduct guidelines among member companies (1975) and a Statement on Corporate Responsibility (1981).

The report is based on information compiled from 100 member companies, listed on the inside back cover. The introductory section examines this information, but the report mainly contains descriptions of ethics policy and practice in 10 companies (Sections 2-11).

> The philosophies, policies and procedures of ten of those companies were studied in detail by specialists in organizational ethics who, in the process, reviewed documents, visited the companies, and interviewed a cross-section of employees in each. The ten companies (Boeing, Champion International, Chemical Bank, General Mills, GTE, Hewlett-Packard, Johnson & Johnson, McDonnell Douglas, Norton, and Xerox) represent a variety in history, industry and geography. The findings of the specialists form the body of the report....(p. 4)

Each company is covered in a separate report that appears as a section of the book, along with the name(s) of the researchers/authors. Also given at the end of each report is a note indicating the source for more information or materials available, with the name of the contact person, address, and phone number (in most instances). The latter, a seemingly minor convenience item, demonstrates a high degree of commitment by the respective companies toward the attainment of "...the hope and intention of The Business Roundtable that the information in this report will be helpful to all corporations seeking to develop, improve, refine, and review their efforts toward more ethical policies and conduct throughout their organizations." (p. 4)

Five researchers/research teams or organizations participated. Each covered two companies, as follows:

Kirk O. Hanson, Stanford Graduate School of Business, and Manuel Velasquez, Santa Clara University: "The Boeing Company: Managing Ethics and Values" (pp. 11-20)
"Hewlett-Packard Company: Managing Ethics and Values" (pp. 65-76)

Kenneth R. Andrews, Emeritus Professor of Business Administration, Harvard Business School: "Ethics in Policy and Practice at General Mills" (pp. 41-52)
"Ethics in Policy and Practice at GTE Corporation" (pp. 53-64)

Charles S. McCoy and Fred N. Twining, Center for Ethics and Social Policy, Berkeley: "The Corporate Values Program at Champion International Corporation" (pp. 21-30)
"The Corporate Ethics Program at the McDonnell Douglas Corporation" (pp. 105-114)

The Ethics Resource Center, Inc., Washington, D.C.: "Chemical Bank Programs in Business Ethics and Corporate Responsibility" (pp. 31-40)
"Xerox Programs in Business Ethics and Corporate Responsibility" (pp. 130-138)

Laura L. Nash, Ph.D., Nash Associates, Cambridge, MA: "Johnson & Johnson's Credo" (pp. 76-104)
"The Norton Company's Ethics Program" (pp. 115-130)

In general, each presentation gives a comprehensive organizational and behavioral profile of the company and the ethical convictions and concerns of its top management. The presentations also provide valuable insights as to the basic innovative and evolutionary processes, interactive human and situational forces, and the role of implementation (enforcement) programs and efforts. The focus is on the principles and the activism in their application and interpretation under various, and varying, conditions, internal and external.

The introductory section, organized as "Lessons that can be learned," also serves as a summary of the book. The lessons are presented under five headings:

1. The Role of Top Management — Commitment, Leadership, Example,
2. Importance of a "Code" — Clarity of Expectations,
3. The Process of Implementation — Making Ethics Work,
4. Involvement and Commitment of Personnel at All Levels,
5. Measuring Results.

Those five lessons are followed by "Conclusion: Self-interest, survival and achievement require attention to corporate ethics." The last paragraph, on p. 10, is quoted below:

> Effective leadership by the management of corporations is the best way to support and advance the cause of private enterprises. Basic to such leadership is the insight that corporate ethics is a strategic key to survival and profitability in this era of fierce competitiveness in a global economy.

Appendix B-5

Toward a Code of Ethics for Management Accountants. C. Mike Merz and David F. Groebner. National Association of Accountants, Montvale, NJ, 1981.

The researchers reviewed the literature on ethics, examined codes of ethics in various professions, and conducted a three-phase survey of NAA members. This study was initiated to help NAA decide what posture, if any, to take with respect to ethics for management accountants. The findings favor a code of ethics.

As to the principal ethical theories, utilitarianism and Kantian, the influence of the former prevails in the United States, in one or another of its versions: act utilitarianism and rule utilitarianism. "Although act utilitarianism seems to be the main ethical basis for democracy and business, many ethical dilemmas have been resolved by applying rule utilitarianism, which asserts that the greatest good results when people consistently follow established rules. Thus, a firm precedent exists in ethical theory for establishing a code of ethics." (p. 12)

The authors point out that established laws already have addressed several areas of possible ethical dilemmas likely to be encountered by management accountants, because most of them work as employees. *The Restatement of Agency* (American Law Institute, 1958) is cited in the report with respect to agent and employee duties and the limitations on those duties — obedience, loyalty, and confidentiality.

In the course of the survey phase of the research, 749 NAA members participated (137 were interviewed in 30 unstructured and 107 structured interviews), and 612 NAA members completed a mail questionnaire. The related documents and analyses appear in four appendices. Though few participants or respondents experienced serious ethical dilemmas in their professional work, most of them tended to favor a code of ethics.

Appendix C

Collections of Studies

Appendix C-1

Research in Corporate Social Performance and Policy, A Research Manual — Empirical Studies of Business Ethics and Values, Volume 9, 1987. William C. Frederick, guest editor, and Lee E. Preston, series editor. JAI Press Inc., Greenwich, CT, 1987.

Business ethics is getting considerable attention these days, both as a research subject and as a topic of news coverage in the media. The latter seems to be a relatively new development, probably associated with the increasing frequency of revelations concerning various deals and behavioral patterns of the prominent and/or notorious players in the ethics-sensitive spheres of corporate and investment activities. The increased coverage accorded this subject area by the media adds a significant dimension to the ongoing debates and analyses. It provides a greater degree of exposure, which, in turn, leads to a broader public awareness of the associated problems, issues, and effects, as well as to a better understanding and recognition of the related constructive efforts, including those of academic and professional researchers.

Consider, for example, the coverage of this book in *The Wall Street Journal* (October 9, 1987, p. 27) in "Nature or Nurture? Study Blames Ethical Lapses on Corporate Goals," by Rick Wartzman, staff reporter. Along with the exposition of the book, the write-up is laced with comments from various sources, including the researchers. A few quotes are given below:

> A quick and easy recipe for corporate virtue has long been the common one: Stir up a code of ethics and sprinkle the firm with a few outside directors renowned for their community concern. But a fresh look at data culled from 10 academic studies suggests that these actions merely

127

pay lip service to a larger — and clearly unmet — problem: a business climate that condones malfeasance. Indeed, the studies together indicate that even the most upright people are apt to become dishonest and unmindful of their civic responsibilities when placed in a typical corporate environment.

The culprit is not personal values, but corporate culture, says William Frederick, a business professor at the University of Pittsburgh, who has put the findings together...

While Mr. Frederick's conclusion isn't entirely novel, using statistics to try and prove it is unprecedented, and corporate consultants say they welcome the work as supporting evidence derived from their own experience.

In his Introduction, Professor Frederick states the criteria the contributors of "the essays in this volume" were asked to meet, refers to the complexities and limitations of research of this type, and identifies some of the main insights and contributions. He and James Weber wrote one of the 10 essays, "The Values of Corporate Managers and Their Critics: An Empirical Description and Normative Implications." (pp. 131-152) Each essay is followed by a list of references, which, all together, add up to a rich set of bibliographical items.

The data used in the first essay, "A Survey and Critique of Business Ethics Research, 1986," by John E. Fleming, were obtained from structured interviews with "more than fifty scholars." (p. 2) Sixteen were directors of business ethics centers. A list of the centers appears in the Appendix on pp. 22-23.

As to the other nine essays, two are on topics directly related to our research project: "A Theory and Measure of Ethical Climate in Organizations," by Bart Victor and John B. Cullen, and "Codes of Ethics: Organizational Behavior and Misbehavior," by M. Cash Matthews. The former applies various analytical approaches to the data gathered from four groups of employees who responded to a questionnaire, in order to develop suitable methods of classification and the ethical climate measures. The latter examines the impact of codes of ethics by comparing illegalities in corporations with and without a code. A content analysis of the codes is included. "The principal finding is that there is little relationship between codes of conduct and corporation violations, contrary to the notion that the codes serve as an effective form of self-regulation."(p. 125) At one point in the concluding portion, the author observes, "To change the behavior patterns requires changing the corporate culture, and the codes are one step in that direction. (p. 127)

One of the essays, "Moral Reasoning in Work-Related Conflicts," by Robin Derry, on pp. 25-49, reports on the on-site structured interviews at a manufacturing facility of a *Fortune* 100 industrial corporation. The interviews were conducted with 40 individuals — 20 women and 20 men — all at the first level of managers and staff professionals. The author concludes that "the two modes of moral reasoning, justice and care, are not gender related. In the corporate setting those differences were not in existence. This may indicate that if such gender differences do exist in the general population, they are not so deeply ingrained that they cannot be adapted or altered to fit the requirements of a strong organizational culture...." (p. 45) Those findings seem to support the view that the state of the corporate ethical climate may have large-scale consequences in a variety of ethics-related situations.

The remaining six essays not explicitly referred to above are: "Illegal Corporate Behavior and the Question of Moral Agency: An Empirical Examination," by P. L. Cochran and D. Nigh; "Illegal Corporate Behavior and Corporate Board Structure," by F. H. Gautschi, III and T. M. Jones; "The Values of Corporate Managers and Their Critics: An Empirical Description and Normative Implications," by W. C. Frederick and J. Weber; "Issues in Work Values Measurement," by E. C. Ravlin and B. M. Meglino; "Cognitive Ability Tests in Employment: Ethical Perspectives of Employers and Society," by J. D. Olian and J. P. Guthrie; and "The Relation of Employee Assistance Programs to Corporate Social Responsibility Attitudes: An Empirical Study," by P. M. Roman and T. C. Blum.

Appendix C-2

"Organizational Culture." Cornell University, Ithaca, NY, 1983. *Administrative Science Quarterly*, Vol. 28, No. 3, September 1983, pp. 331-502.

An overview of the articles is presented in "Introduction: A Code of Many Colors," by M. Jelinek, L. Smircich, and P. Hirsch. This special issue of the Quarterly comprises the papers selected from "some 60 papers" received in response to a call for manuscripts. "The nine papers...all focus on culture as an interpretive framework for sense making (by both members and others) in organizational settings." (p. 332) As to the Commonalities and Distinctions, "Most of the papers presented here, despite their variety, share a processual view of culture as the continuous recreation of shared meanings....Culture is intersubjective and simultaneously cause and effect, for most of these papers...." (pp. 335-6) As to the Directions for Future Research, "Of considerably less visibility here are the outcomes in terms of organizational performance, responsiveness to change, or results...." (pp. 337-8)

L. Smircich in "Concepts of Culture and Organizational Analysis" (pp. 339-358) says, "This paper in particular traces the ways culture has been developed in organization studies: as a critical variable and as a root metaphor....This paper examines the assumptions that underlie the different ways the concept of culture has been used in organization studies." (pp. 339-40) A sampling of the research on organizational culture shows: "Overall, the research agenda...is how to mold and shape internal culture in particular ways...consistent with managerial purposes." (p. 346)

K.L.Gregory, the author of "Native-View Paradigms: Multiple Cultures and Culture Conflicts in Organizations" (pp. 359-376), describes and critiques holistic paradigms in many studies on corporate cultures and points out that they are not substantially different from earlier Human Relations approaches. She uses the results of a recent ethnographic study to "discover native views in Silicon Valley" where "occupational communities" tend to hold contrasting views with conflicting cultures within the same company.

The authors of "The Uniqueness Paradox in Organizational Stories," J. Martin, M. S. Feldman, M. J. Hatch, and S. B. Sitkin (pp. 438-453), argue that corporate claims to uniqueness — that one is unlike any other — are, paradoxically, expressed through cultural manifestations, such as stories, that are not in fact unique.

The article "Communication to Self in Organizations and Cultures," by H. Broms and H. Gahmberg (pp. 482-495), begins as follows: "In 1979 we made a computer search...and found about 50 business articles with the word myth in them. In late 1981...the same sources gave more than 500 articles!" (p. 482). The authors examine various sources and forms of mythology of oneself or of an organization.

The remaining five articles are: "A Rumplestiltskin Organization: Metaphors on Metaphors in Field Research," by K. K. Smith and V. M. Simmons; "Semiotics and Study of Occupational and Organizational Cultures," by S. R. Barley; "A Structurationist Account of Political Cultures," by P. Riley; "Transaction Costs, Property Rights, and Organizational Culture: An Exchange Perspective," by G. R. Jones; and "Efficient Cultures: Exploring the Relationship between Culture and Organizational Performance," by A. L. Wilkins and W. G. Ouchi.